Mitchell Symons was born in London and educated at Mill Hill School and the LSE, where he studied law. Since leaving BBC TV, where he was a researcher and then a director, he has worked as a writer, broadcaster and journalist. He was a principal writer of early editions of the board game Trivial Pursuit and has devised many television formats. He is also the author of more than fifty books, and currently writes a weekly column for the Sunday Express. *Why Eating Bogeys Is Good For You* won the Blue Peter Best Book with Facts Award in 2010 and he repeated this success with *Do Igloos Have Loos?* in 2011.

www.**grossbooks**.co.uk

How much yucky stuff do you know?

Collect all these gross fact books by Mitchell Symons!

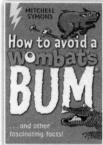

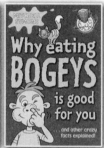

Available now!

Why Spacemen can't BURP

Mitchell Symons

DOUBLEDAY

WHY SPACEMEN CAN'T BURP
A DOUBLEDAY BOOK 978 0 857 53097 4

Published in Great Britain by Doubleday, an imprint of
Random House Children's Publishers UK
A Random House Group Company

This edition published 2013

1 3 5 7 9 10 8 6 4 2

Copyright © Mitchell Symons, 2013
Illustrations copyright © Nigel Baines, 2013

The right of Mitchell Symons to be identified as the author
of this work has been asserted in accordance with the Copyright,
Designs and Patents Act 1988.

The Random House Group Limited supports the Forest Stewardship Council®
(FSC®), the leading international forest-certification organisation. Our books
carrying the FSC label are printed on FSC®-certified paper. FSC is the only
forest-certification scheme supported by the leading environmental organisations,
including Greenpeace. Our paper procurement policy can be found at
www.randomhouse.co.uk/environment

RANDOM HOUSE CHILDREN'S PUBLISHERS UK
61–63 Uxbridge Road, London W5 5SA

Set in Optima

www.**randomhousechildrens**.co.uk
www.**randomhouse.co**.uk

Addresses for companies within The Random House Group Limited
can be found at: www.**randomhouse**.co.uk/offices.htm
THE RANDOM HOUSE GROUP Limited Reg. No. 954009

A CIP catalogue record for this book is available from the British Library.

Printed and bound in Great Britain by Clays Ltd, St Ives plc

To my great nephews
Dominic, Oliver and Harry
and to my great-niece Alyssia

Introduction

OK, regular readers (and a big welcome back to you!) will have got the drill by now. This is a question-and-answer book, like *Why Eating Bogeys Is Good for You*, which provided the answers to questions like, *Do identical twins have identical fingerprints? Why is the sea blue? Is it cheaper to send yourself as a parcel to Australia rather than flying on an aeroplane? Can you knock yourself out using just your own fist? What happens to a cow if you don't milk it? Why would anyone want to pop a weasel?* and, yes, *Why is eating bogeys good for you?*

After *Why Do Farts Smell Like Rotten Eggs?* and *Do Igloos Have Loos?* which answered a huge number of similar questions between them, I thought we might have covered everything. But that was to reckon without my readers and friends who, between them, came up with some real posers!

Questions in this book include: *Is there any dog in a hot dog? Is it true that there's a special chemical used in swimming pools that*

turns the water green if someone pees in it?
Is it possible to keep a fox as a pet? Who was
Good King Wenceslas – as in the carol – and
was he really good? Why does the leaning
tower of Pisa lean? What's the hardest thing
for a ventriloquist to say? Why are very young
children called 'infants'? How many people
does a whale have to kill before it's a killer
whale? Why do we cross our fingers for luck?
How deserted does land have to be before
it's known as a desert? Why is it always Dad
who does the barbecue? Is there anything that
children can do better than adults?
Could a (human) child ever be raised by
animals? Why is Father Christmas also known
as Santa Claus? Why are baked beans always
sold in tomato sauce? Who sent the very first
tweet on Twitter? Is it ever acceptable to use
the word 'ain't'? If all the animals went into
Noah's ark two by two, wouldn't they have
eaten one another? When will the world end?
Why do mosquito bites itch? Has an animal
ever been fitted with glasses? Why do round
pizzas come in square boxes? Has anyone
ever swum from one continent to another?
Are Brussels sprouts Belgian? Why do bruises
change colour? Has the queen ever been to

McDonald's? How can I tell if someone is lying to me?

Once again, where possible, I went to experts for the answers. My thanks to them all. I also used my large library of reference books as well as the internet (although I tried to use this to check facts rather than, as is so tempting, as a tool of first resort). So I would like to take this opportunity to thank all the extremely clever people who helped me to answer these extraordinary questions.

Now for some even more important acknowledgements because without these people, this book couldn't have been written at all: (in alphabetical order): my fantastic editor Lauren Buckland, my wife and chief researcher Penny Chorlton, my lovely publisher Annie Eaton, and the designers Rachel Lawston and Nigel Baines.

In addition, I'd also like to thank the following people for their help, contributions and/or support: Gilly Adams, Luigi Bonomi, Paul Donnelley, Jonathan Fingerhut, Jenny Garrison, Philip Garrison, Bryn Musson, Nicholas Ridge,

Mari Roberts, Charlie Symons, Jack Symons, Louise Symons, David Thomas, Martin Townsend, Louise Vallant, Clair Woodward and Rob Woolley.

If I've missed anyone out, then please know that – as with any mistakes in the book – it is, as I always say, entirely down to my own stupidity.

Mitchell Symons

Is it true that there's a special chemical used in swimming pools that turns the water green if someone pees in it?

. . . or blue or red or, indeed, yellow!

No there isn't.
But I've heard . . .
No there isn't!
But my friend tells me . . .

Look, how many times do I have to tell you that there really isn't a special chemical that changes the colour of swimming-pool water when someone pees. Well, apart from the 'chemical' we scientists call 'wee-wee'.

So why do so many people think there is?
It's all a clever con trick played by the people who own or run swimming pools. Obviously they don't want any wee in their pools and so they tell people that there's a chemical in the water that will turn the water a different colour if someone wees. But it's not true! There isn't

any such chemical. They just want you to think
there is to stop you from weeing in the pool.
Aha, you think, well that means I can now wee
in the pool.
No it doesn't!

The reason NOT to wee in the pool is that it's absolutely gross and totally unnecessary (there are toilets for that sort of thing) not because you might get caught out by some non-existent chemical.

You can, however, have a wee in the sea: there's nothing wrong with that but NEVER, NEVER, NEVER in a pool.

What's the most extraordinary escape a prisoner has ever made?

Gosh, that's a difficult question!

There were many brave and ingenious escapes (and escape attempts) by prisoners-of-war in both World War One and (especially) World War Two. Extraordinarily complex tunnels were dug using little more than knives and forks that had been adapted for the purpose. These escapes were all the more remarkable because the men attempting them knew that they were risking their lives; they would almost certainly be shot if they were discovered in the act of escaping.

But I'm going to pick a Mafia gangster named Vincenzo Curcio who, in the year 2000, escaped from an Italian prison by sawing through the bars of his cell. So far, so unremarkable, but what made this escape so utterly unbelievable was his choice of tool. He didn't use a saw, he didn't even use a knife: he used . . . wait for it . . . dental floss. That's right: dental floss! That stuff you use – or you should use but you don't bother until the day before your next dental appointment – to clean in between your teeth; that stuff that breaks the moment in comes into contact with even your least snaggly tooth; that stuff you wouldn't have thought was capable of cutting marshmallow in half, was the tool that Curcio chose to cut through his cell window bars and then escape from the prison with sheets knotted together.

Now, at this point I should say that the prison had been built to stop people breaking in rather than breaking out and so the bars were

made of steel low in carbon, which made them more ductile (i.e. easier to saw through). But, even so, what an amazing achievement!

The upshot of the whole story is that the enterprising Curcio was caught less than four months later and sent back to prison.

But don't feel sorry for him because he was a murderer who deserved to be behind bars – especially ones he couldn't saw his way through!

In other words, we applaud his inventiveness, but crime does NOT pay!

How can I tell if someone is lying to me?

It's difficult, isn't it? Of course, if it's a politician, you can tell they're lying just because their mouth is open.

Kidding aside, it's hard to tell – which is why psychologists have made several studies.

Here are some of their tips to help you . . .

- Physical expression will be limited and stiff, with few arm and hand movements.
- Hand, arm and leg movements are towards their own body as the liar tries to take up less space.
- They'll touch their face, throat, nose or mouth but are unlikely to touch their chest or heart with an open hand.
- People who are lying to you tend to look up and to their left.

- Liars will also avoid making eye contact. Instead, they concentrate almost exclusively on what their mouth is doing.

- Interestingly, their timing is often awry. In other words, what they say and do aren't properly synchronized. For example, you'll hand someone a present and they'll say they love it but they'll smile after making that statement and not at the same time. Alternatively, their words and gestures are at odds. So they'll say 'I like you' and frown – instead of smile – when then say it.
- Liars might place objects (books, mugs or toys) between themselves and you.
- A liar will use your words to answer a question. So if you asked someone 'Did you eat my sweets?' and they answer 'No, I did not eat your sweets' then they might very well be lying. Whereas, if they reply, 'No, I didn't' then they're probably telling the truth.

But the best sign that someone is lying is that they talk too much. Liars aren't comfortable with silence or pauses in the conversation and so they try to fill them with any old words.

Why do Americans write the date a different way from us?

I was born on 11 February 1957 (and do please keep those birthday cards coming in). When I express this in figures, I write it as 11/2/1957 – like any British person would: day/month/ year. Americans, however, would write it as 2/11/1957 – i.e. month/day/year.

Obviously, when the day is greater than twelve (the total number of months) then there's no confusion: 9/17/1963 couldn't be anything other than September 9 as there isn't a 17th month in the year.

However, with a date where the day is lower than twelve, it can be very confusing.

To an American, I was born on November 2nd and while I would like to be a bit younger, I don't like confusion.

So why do the Americans do it the wrong way round?

Well, it turns out that they don't. They do it the right way round!

In the 18th century, British newspapers always wrote the month first and then the date. So it was, for example, October 19 1785 rather than 19 October 1785 and the Americans merely continued this way of doing things when they shortened the date to numbers only.
It was we British who are to blame for switching the day and the month around.
In fact, if you take a look at a British newspaper (as I've just done), you'll see that the date is always written with the month first.

Has the Queen ever been to McDonald's?

I'm not asking for your sympathy, I'm really not, but honestly, the things I have to do for you!

Well, when I say 'you', I really mean a young reader named Alfie who asked me this question.

I suppose I should be flattered that Alfie has enough confidence in my investigative abilities to find the answer to his query, but I have to tell you that it led to quite a lot of head scratching on my part.

My first port of call was McDonald's head office but they had no idea whatsoever. 'So,' I said with a bit of a sneer in my voice, 'you don't keep a record of every person who eats in your restaurants?'

'Er, no. Would you expect us to?' McDonald's 1, Mitchie 0.

I tried the internet, but that didn't really help – although it did reveal that Her Majesty actually owns a McDonald's (well, sort of).

According to a news report from 2008, 'Among Her Majesty's most recent acquisitions was a retail park in Slough – which encompasses a drive-through McDonald's. Bath Road Retail Park was purchased this month by the Crown Estate, which administers the monarch's property portfolio, for £92 million.

The site, which is visible from the Queen's
State Apartments at Windsor Castle, is also
home to a B&Q superstore, and branches of
Comet, JJB Sports and Mothercare.'

So far so good, but I was still a Happy Meal
short of an answer – and discovering that
Princes William and Harry had both been
through the Golden Arches wasn't helping me
get any further in my quest.

Nor did a rumour I saw on various sites that
Her Majesty 'might' have once sent out for a
Big Mac just to see what they were like.
No, there was nothing else for it. I was going to
have to phone her myself.

Yes, that's right, I, Mitchell Symons, the author
of such books as *How to Avoid a Wombat's
Bum, How Much Poo Does an Elephant Do?*
and *Why Does Ear Wax Taste So Gross?* was
going to ask our esteemed Head of State
whether she had ever eaten in McDonald's.
Yeah right. Of course I did. Because I want
to spend the rest of (what remains of) my life
in the Tower. Which is almost certainly the
punishment for bothering our monarch with

totally fatuous questions. (*They don't put people in the Tower any more – Editor*). I know, I know, but I still don't think I'll take the chance.

So, as a compromise, I phoned the Buckingham Palace press office. A very posh sounding man answered the phone.
'Hello, can I help you?'

Er, yes, my name is Mitchell Symons. I write books for children (I gave him some of the titles). You can look me up on Google.

'Ha ha, yes, I see. Well, what can I do for you?'

I just wondered if the Queen has ever eaten in McDonald's? It's not me who wants to know but a lad named Alfie.

'I'm sorry, I really can't comment on that.'

Couldn't you ask Her Majesty?

There was a silence on the other end of the line, which I felt obliged to break. 'I understand,' I said, 'you don't fancy risking your job by asking silly questions.'

He sounded relieved. *'Something like that.'*
I thanked him and rang off. He kept his job and
I kept my head (*They really don't chop your
head off for bothering the Queen – Editor*). As
for poor Alfie, well I'm sorry to fail him, truly I
am, but I think we're both going to have to live
our lives without knowing for sure whether our
Queen has been to a McDonald's or not.

. . . and following on from that, is it really true that there has never been a war between two countries that both have McDonald's?

Alas it isn't.

I suppose this is an extension of the line that
no two (fully functioning) democracies have
ever gone to war with each other. That is true –
though only by applying the 'fully functioning'
test (i.e. by establishing that both countries have
independent courts and judges as well as totally
free and fair elections).

The McDonald's 'fact' isn't – despite the fact that there has been plenty written about 'the McDonald's effect': the idea being that two countries that had McDonald's would be civilized enough not to engage in warfare. See the Democratic Peace Theory and the Golden Arches Theory of Conflict Resolution.

In fact, Georgia and Russia – both of which have McDonald's – have engaged in a war with each other while Israel and Lebanon's conflict wasn't helped by the fact that their citizens were all able to enjoy McMeals. It's a shame, isn't it?

How do you get a 'sense of direction'?

Biologically, a good sense of direction is based on your ability to take advantage of environmental clues. Skilled navigators mentally update their geographical position by keeping track of visual evidence, such as trees or distant views and the angles to them. Such abilities are the result of observation, training and practice – often from a young age – rather than a superhuman talent for getting from A to B. Neurologists (doctors who study the nervous system) agree that deliberately noting landmarks and turns as you move around should help you to build your mental map of an area.

My wife, Penny, has a good sense of direction because, as a child, she used to ride her horse around the woods and the Sussex South Downs on her own. Mind you, she is lost in cities as her navigational skills require trees and other natural markers. But the same rules apply in urban areas: you just have to memorize different things – landmarks that won't change, like churches, road signs, bends in unmarked roads, that sort of thing.

My sister Jenny, a great girl in every other respect, has absolutely no sense of direction and can't even use a map. Before getting a sat nav, she used to measure her journeys by the number of 'excuse me's' she had to say when asking people for help!

Mitch to Jenny: How was your journey to Blackpool yesterday?

Jenny to Mitch: Not so bad. It only took twelve 'scuse me's!

Why can't children vote?

In Britain, everyone can vote in local and Parliamentary elections – everyone, that is, except the Queen, members of the House of Lords, the insane and people who are in prison (although there are moves to make changes there). Oh, but there is one rule: you have to be over 18.

It hasn't always been that way. Go back in time to before the First World War and only men could vote. Before the electoral reform acts of 1832 and 1867, only (male) homeowners and/or landowners could vote.

Over the centuries, the right to vote has been extended to almost everyone . . . almost everyone, that is, except YOU.

So why can't children vote?
WHY?

The reason it's 18 is because that's the age of adulthood. When the age of adulthood – or 'majority' as it's known – was 21 (prior to

1970) then that was the minimum voting age. There's a good argument for maintaining 18 at the age at which you can vote. If you're an adult, then you have all the rights of an adult, but also all of the responsibilities. Why should a child be able to vote when they don't have all these responsibilities?

You don't pay tax so why should you be able to vote to decide how that tax should be spent? Also, or so it is argued, children don't understand all the issues.
WHY NOT?
If the argument for 18 is that adults have all sorts of responsibilities – especially the responsibility of paying tax – then what about all those adults who don't have those responsibilities? Students, the unemployed etc. – they're all allowed to vote; so why shouldn't you?

As for not understanding the issues, there are plenty of ignorant adults and just as many more intelligent children.

Why not lower the age from 18 to 11? Perhaps there could be some sort of reasoning test

for children before they're allowed to vote. But I can't see any reason why the right (and responsibility) to vote shouldn't be given to children.

After all, you're the people who have to live with the consequences of what politicians do today. So maybe those politicians should be accountable to you.

It's worth thinking about!

Who sent the very first tweet on Twitter?

No, it wasn't Stephen Fry! Even though he was responsible – in this country at least – for an enormous surge in Twitter's popularity, he wasn't the very first tweeter.

Nope, that honour, appropriately enough, belongs to Jack Dorsey, the man who created Twitter.

Having come up with the idea of someone being able to communicate with a small group

via an SMS message, on 21 March 2006,
Dorsey published the first Twitter message: 'Just
setting up my twttr'.

Here I should explain that the original project
code name for the service was 'twttr', which
was inspired by Flickr and the five-character
length of American SMS short codes. This was
expanded to 'twitter' which was defined as 'a
short burst of inconsequential information',
and 'chirps from birds'. According to Dorsey
'that's exactly what the product was.'
Twitter was introduced publicly on 15 July
2006 and has been a major social networking
tool ever since.

Why do dogs put their tails between their legs?

. . . especially when they're being told
off! There's a very good reason for it:
embarrassment – a bit like you or I might put a
hand in front of our face.

What you have to know is that dogs' most

powerful sense is smell. That's why they sniff each other's bottoms. When a dog puts its tail between its legs it is, effectively, covering its bottom so that no one else – and certainly not the person telling it off (whom they see as a pack leader) – can sniff their bum!

Who was Good King Wenceslas – as in the carol – and was he really good?

For a start, Wenceslas wasn't a king, he was a duke! To be specific, he was a Bohemian duke who lived in the 10th century. He was killed by his brother who was opposed to Wenceslas's Christian beliefs and so became the patron saint of Bohemians. Today, he is the patron saint of the Czech Republic (which includes the region of Bohemia).

After his death, the Holy Roman Emperor declared that he should have a more 'regal dignity and title'. In other words, it would be better to refer to him as a prince or even as a king rather than as a 'mere' duke – out of respect to his Christian devotion. And that's why the carol is called Good King Wenceslas.

The carol itself is interesting because it suggests that Wenceslas was able to miraculously warm the snow while he was out and about giving 'alms' (charitable gifts) to the poor on Boxing Day (26 December).

Not sure about that – but I do know it's an excellent carol to sing (even if it was only very recently that I learned that the carol starts 'Good King Wenceslas looked out, on the Feast of Stephen' and not – as I had always thought – 'Good King Wences last looked out . . .' oops!) So was he 'good'? Well, in those days, 'goodliness' and 'Godliness' were seen as exactly the same thing and he was certainly full of Godliness. From what I've read about

him, my guess is that, by the standards of the times he lived in, he was a good man. And, besides, all those Bohemians obviously thought so . . . and who are we to disagree?

How did the beefeaters get their name?

Beefeaters, the people who wear striking dark blue and red uniforms and guard the Tower of London, got their name because . . . they used to eat a lot of beef.

Yup, it's as simple as that.

Beefeaters, more properly called Yeoman Warders, were given the right to eat beef from the king's table. A seventeenth century Italian visitor commented that 'A very large ration of beef is given to them daily at court . . . that they might be called Beef-eaters.' But the name 'beefeater' was probably first used as an insult by the frequently starving inhabitants of London who may well have taunted the Warders with the name as a reference to the fact that they got preferential treatment from the Crown and received beef to eat when others had to do without.

Is it true that Sir Isaac Newton discovered gravity when an apple fell on his head?

You must know the story. Sir Isaac Newton, the great physicist, was sitting underneath an apple tree when an apple fell on his head prompting him to come up with his theory of gravity.

So did this really happen?
Alas, it didn't.

Of course, we all like to think that such stories are true because it appeals to our love of stories. The idea that a clever person only comes up with their brilliant theory as a result of something totally mundane happening to them is always appealing. Whether it's Archimedes in his bath, Alexander Fleming and his dirty dish or Newton and his apple,

it tickles us to think that, when it comes to the really important discoveries, they don't take place in laboratories but in everyday circumstances.
So how did this myth arise?

In fact, it came about because of something someone wrote some sixty years after Newton's death: 'Whilst he was musing in a garden it came into his thought that the power of gravity (which brought an apple from the tree to the ground) was not limited to a certain distance from the earth but that this power must extend much further.'

From here, you can see how and why a complex theory could have been reduced to what is little more than a fairy tale.

Is it ever acceptable to use the word ain't'?

Many people will tell you that it is NEVER acceptable to use the word ain't as it's slang. Well, they're wrong!

Although it is sometimes – in fact, almost always – used as slang, there is one example I'm going to give you where it's not only acceptable, but also absolutely correct.
OK, so let's start with how it's used in slang. 'He ain't coming' someone will say of a friend who has decided not to turn up somewhere, when what they mean to say is 'He isn't coming'. Or they'll say 'There ain't no time for that' when they're in a hurry – rather than 'There isn't any time for that'.

So where can it be used – legitimately and properly?

The answer is as a contraction (a shortening) of the words 'am not'. In other words, wherever you would use the words 'am not' or 'am I not', you can use the word ain't instead. In fact, it would be wrong not to!

Let me give you an example. Let's take the following expression: 'I'm a good person, aren't I?'

That's wrong . . . it should be 'I'm a good

person, ain't I?'
Why?

Because 'aren't I' is a contraction of 'are not I'. Well, you don't say 'I are a good person', do you? So you shouldn't say, 'I'm a good person, are not I'.

'I'm a good person, ain't I' works because it's a quicker way of saying 'I'm a good person, am not I' and that, dear reader, is absolutely correct!

Why do brides have bridesmaids?

Principally, to attend to the bride – much in the same way that the best man would look after the groom. Traditionally, the most senior bridesmaid would help prepare the flowers, decorate the tables for the wedding feast and help dress the bride.

However, there is one tradition from ancient Rome that continues to the present day: the one in which bridesmaids all wear identical

dresses. This is a clear echo of Roman law, which required ten witnesses at a wedding in order to outsmart evil spirits (believed to attend marriage ceremonies) by dressing in identical clothing to the bride and groom, so that the evil spirits wouldn't know who was getting married.

Nowadays, of course, the bride wears different clothes from her bridesmaids, but they are all dressed alike – as are the groom and his supporters.

The power of superstition!

If I eat lots of spinach, will I be as strong as Popeye?

Popeye, as all his fans will remember, was a weak sailor until, fuelled by a tin of spinach, he gained sufficient strength to beat up Bluto and rescue Olive Oyl (oops, I've just spoilt the plot of just about every single Popeye cartoon ever made!).

But why spinach?

Because it was thought to contain huge
amounts of iron which, in turn, was thought to

endow strength.
The only problem was that, even if iron alone
could make you strong (which it can't), spinach

doesn't have a huge amount of iron. The reason why people thought it did was because of a simple mistake by a Doctor von Wolff who wrote a paper in 1870 about the benefits of the vegetable and listed its iron content. Unfortunately, he put a decimal point in the wrong place so that it appeared as if spinach contained ten times more iron than it actually did. Honestly, I'm not making this up! The mistake wasn't corrected until 1937. In fact, spinach isn't an especially good source of iron but it does contain important vitamins and other good things. So do eat it, but don't be fooled into thinking it'll make you strong!

If all the animals went into Noah's ark – two by two – wouldn't they have eaten one another?

Almost certainly – and that's not the only implausibility about Noah's Ark. Apart from anything, it would have had to have been a

pretty big ark to hold them all!
I think, as with the story of Adam and Eve,
it's impossible to take this story literally.
Irrespective of your religious beliefs, it simply
couldn't have happened as described in the
Bible although – again, as with Adam and Eve
– it works as a cautionary tale. Behave yourself
and do as you're told and you'll be fine.

As the father of two sons, I can attest to the
importance of controlling people's behaviour!

One thing though. While considering this
question, I did a little research and discovered
that it's even more unlikely than I'd first
thought. In fact, according to the Bible, the
'clean' (according to Jewish dietary laws)
animals boarded the ark in groups of seven: it
was only the unclean animals that went on in
groups of two. Since there are far more clean
animals than unclean, most of the animals
would have gone on in groups of seven. Which
would have made it even more crowded than
it would otherwise have been.

Yup, and increased the chances of animals
eating one another . . .

When does a shower become rain?

I must confess that until I looked into this, I always thought of a shower as a short spell of light rain and rain itself as something that goes on for some time (usually all day).

It turns out I couldn't have been more wrong. According to the meteorologist I asked, a shower can last as long as 'rain' and be just as light or heavy. The difference is that the word 'shower' applies to a much smaller area. So if your local area has rain while it's dry in nearby areas, then it's a shower. But if there's rain over a much larger area then it isn't a 'shower' but 'rain'.

I think the confusion comes about because we often talk about 'a short shower', which makes us think of showers as always being short rather than being of any duration, but always local.

Why, if you buy something sub-standard, are you said to have been 'sold a pup'?

Picture the scene. I come back from the mobile phone shop absolutely thrilled with (what I think is) the very latest telephone. My son, who knows far more about these things than I will ever know, says, 'Oh dear, Dad, you've bought something that's at least two months out of date . . . they've sold you a pup'. In other words, the shop managed to offload an older inferior phone on to an unsuspecting customer. This goes back to the times when people didn't buy meat – they bought animals.

So you'd go to the market and buy a piglet, which the salesman would put in a sack. Sometimes, if you were distracted, an unscrupulous salesman would slip a puppy into the sack instead of a piglet (puppies being worth a lot less than piglets). If you were swindled in that way you were said to have been 'sold a pup'.

Why do doughnuts have holes in the middle?

For the same reason that bagels have holes in them: to allow the dough to cook evenly. Without a hole you end up with either a fried ball that is raw in the middle or overcooked on the outside. Instead of a hole, British doughnuts usually have jam in the middle which I have to say is a much better solution

to the problem (though it doesn't explain why the jam always oozes out the other side when I take my first bite).

Which male film star played a female in all his films?

This is a trick question, which I've included because it's a lot of fun and might help you to fool various members of your family!

There used to be a film star named Lassie who starred in a number of films. Lassie was a dog – supposedly a female dog. However all the dogs who played her were male dogs. All in all, nine dogs played Lassie, with Pal, born on 20 June 1940, being the first.

Why can't spacemen burp?

Burping is caused by gas pressure in your tummy. And the trouble is, that in the weightless environment of space (also known as zero gravity), you don't have gravity separating the gas in your stomach from the liquid, making a good old expulsion of air (burp, to you and me) nigh on impossible!

Why, if we do something badly, are we said to have made a pig's ear of it?

This derives from the old proverb 'you can't make a silk purse out of a sow's ear', which dates from the 16th century. A sow is a lady pig! In other words, no matter how skilled you are, if the material you're working with is no good, you won't be able to do very much with it. So if you make a pig's ear of a job or task then you've done it badly.

Why is the Kit Kat chocolate bar so called?

This four-finger confection was initially launched in the UK in September 1935 as 'Rowntree's Chocolate Crisp' and re-named two years later as Kit Kat Chocolate Crisp. It became just Kit Kat after the Second World War. No one is certain where the name came from, but it's thought the famous Kit-Kat Club of the 1920s had some influence.

For most of its life, Kit Kat has appeared in a red and white wrapper. It did, however, change to a blue wrapper in 1942, when it was produced with a plain chocolate covering due to milk shortages during the Second World War. This blue livery was withdrawn in 1949 when the standard milk chocolate Kit Kat was reintroduced.

The traditional bar has four fingers which each measure approximately 1 centimetre (0.39 inches) by 9 centimetres (3.5 inches). A two-finger bar was launched in the 1960s, and has remained the company's best-selling

biscuit brand ever since.

Kit Kat was first advertised on TV back in 1957 and had its first colour advert in 1967. Famous adverts include the 'Have a Break' campaign in the 1990s.

In 2010 a new £5 million manufacturing line was opened by Nestlé in York, UK. This can produce more than a billion Kit Kat bars each year.

Why do we rub the site of the injury when we've bumped into something?

Obviously the first thing you do after bumping into something is to scream. Very loudly. This must help or else why would we do it? Some people swear by swearing too, but then they've probably got potty mouths anyway for, as we know, there's nothing big or clever about swearing (*I can't believe I'm reading this, Mitch: you are the original Mr Potty Mouth – Editor*).

Anyway, after screaming, shouting and, in some people's case, swearing, our next reaction is to rub the part of our body that has been injured.

But why do we do this?

Well, there's a very good reason: rubbing your skin after you bump into something helps to ease the pain because the signals sent to the brain from the rubbing interfere with the pain signals.

You could compare this to the remedy I was offered to counteract the effects of static electricity shocks from car doors – which was to smack the car door.

It was pointed out to me that what I hate about those shocks is not the pain but the shock so, by smacking the car door, I would replace the shock with pain.

Rubbing yourself after a knock is similar: you're trading a sensation (the rubbing) you can handle for one (the pain) that you can't.

Do you have to be Scottish to get off 'scot free'?

No you don't! In fact, this expression – meaning to get away with something, without any punishment – has absolutely nothing to do with Scotland or the Scottish.

The word 'scot' is an old Norse word meaning 'payment' – specifically, a payment made to a landlord or sheriff. So if you were allowed to get away without making a payment, you were literally 'scot free'.

Och, d'ye ken that?

Why do we say that someone who's getting over-excited is 'having kittens'?

This is an expression that's usually applied to a girl or a woman who's angry and/or frightened. 'You'd better come home quickly. You've made a real mess in the kitchen and your mother's having kittens' is a call I can remember getting more than once in my youth.

So where does it come from – and why kittens? You won't be surprised to learn that this goes back to olden days when people believed in witches. If a pregnant woman was experiencing terrible pains, it was thought that a particularly evil witch had cast a spell on the woman and turned the baby in her womb into a litter of kittens scratching at her insides.

It was specifically kittens because cats were the animals most associated with witches (every self-respecting witch had one).

You can see how this would have spread from pregnant women to women generally. Fortunately, pregnant women are looked after a lot better these days!

Why is it that the first smell of a rose is so much more powerful than the second?

Until a reader asked me this question – and please do keep sending me your questions – I hadn't even noticed this but, in fact, it is true. The first smell – of anything – is always so much more pungent or powerful than subsequent smells.

I asked a perfume expert why this should be so and he told me that it's all to do with 'acclimatization'. 'The first smell gives you 90 per cent of what you're going to get from the perfume or flower or whatever it is you're smelling.'

Why?

'Ah,' said my friendly smells expert (which doesn't make him a 'smelly expert'), 'this is where it gets technical. When you smell something, all your olfactory cells – the cells that carry those smells to the brain – are engaged. But once they've sent those messages

to the brain, they've done their work and so don't really bother to do it again. So the first smell really is the most important.'

But you can still smell things after that first smell?

'New things will engage the olfactory cells again but if you go to smell the same thing again, the second smell will yield far less and the third smell less still. It's the brain's way to stop you from continually smelling things that might be noxious. The trouble is that it also stops us from enjoying the scent of a rose beyond the initial sniff.'

Is it possible to keep a fox as a pet?

Despite the fact that foxes are portrayed as ever-so-charming in Disney films, they're really rather anti-social creatures as far as we humans are concerned.

True, some people leave food out for them, but this is not a good idea as it encourages them to breed more, which results in frequent raids on hen houses throughout the country as the ever-growing fox population struggles to find food. But even if a fox keeps returning to a garden to take advantage of people's misguided kindness, it will never let a person come close to it because it is a wild animal and wild animals cannot be domesticated.

They can, however, have the wildness bred out of them. In the case of foxes, if you carried on breeding the tamest of every litter, you would eventually end up with dogs. It takes about 20 years to turn a fox into a dog. In the 1950s, Russian scientist Dmitri Belyaev trapped wild silver foxes and set out to breed them until they became tame. Belyaev only bred from the tamest foxes of each generation.

Gradually, the foxes started to look and behave like domesticated dogs, wagging their tails and developing floppy ears and black and white spotted coats.

In another words, you can't keep a wild fox as a pet, but if you breed foxes, taking the tamest cub and then keep breeding with other very tame cubs then, after several generations, you would indeed have something that you could call a pet.

The only thing is, you wouldn't be able to call it a fox!

Why does the leaning tower of Pisa lean?

Although millions of people travel to Pisa in northern Italy to see the famous leaning tower, it was all an accident!

Work on the tower began in the 12th century. The land under the town has several layers of silt and soft clay. This is what makes the subsoil so unstable and that's why the 15,000-tonne tower tilts or leans. It actually started to lean even when they were still building it.
There are plenty of straight towers that don't attract a tenth of the number of visitors to Pisa. How galling must that be to those towns and shopkeepers who would love to welcome all those tourists who, like me, flock to see a wonky tower!

By the way, if you do go to see the tower – and I would thoroughly recommend it, especially if you combine it with a visit to the beautiful city of Florence – then be sure to take a photo of your mum or dad pretending to hold up the leaning tower and prevent it from falling. It never fails to amuse!

Have you got a story about a politician who died because he didn't wear an overcoat?

Funny you should ask . . .

Let me tell you about William Henry Harrison. William probably deserved his turn as American president. His father, Benjamin, had been one of the signatories of the Declaration of Independence and Governor of Virginia, and William himself was a hero to many Americans because of his exploits with the army. In 1836 he ran for president and was defeated, but in 1840 he won remarkably easily.

By this time, however, he was 68 years old (and the oldest American president ever), which led to people calling him 'Granny Harrison'. To counteract the rumours that he was too old and weak to run the country, he decided not to wear an overcoat when he took the Oath of Office.

This was a big mistake as the ceremony was outside on a bitterly cold day. He then gave the longest inaugural address in American presidential history, which took him nearly two hours to read, before riding though the streets of Washington to meet the people. The end result was that Harrison caught a chill.

With his hectic schedule there was no time for him to rest and the chill rapidly developed into pleurisy and pneumonia. He died just thirty days, eleven hours and thirty minutes after taking office, making his the shortest presidency ever.

And all because he wouldn't wear his coat.

So the next time your mother tells you to put on your coat, just think of poor William Henry Harrison and do precisely what she tells you to!

What are the most valuable postage stamps in the world?

It's impossible to give you a definitive list (and any stamp collectors – or philatelists as they're called – among you will be suitably amused by my use of the word 'definitive' as this is also the word used to describe 'ordinary' stamps).

But here are some of the most extraordinary stamps ever issued.

Let's start with the very first stamp: the Penny Black, which was first issued on 1 May 1840 and first used five days later. People had paid for postage before, but usually when receiving letters rather than sending them. This stamp was used to facilitate the very first universal system of paying for postage beforehand.

The Penny Black isn't a rare stamp – more than 68 million were printed – but there are variations of it (with printing errors) that are valuable. Stamps are printed in sheets and the only known complete sheets of the Penny Black are owned by the British Postal Museum.

However, Sweden's very first stamp, the Treskilling Yellow, issued in 1855, is exceptionally valuable and, at the time of writing, holds the world record auction sales price for a single postage stamp. Incredibly, I can't tell you how much that was – though it was certainly more than the £1.5 million it had previously sold for – because the price wasn't revealed and all the bidders were sworn to secrecy!

There's one stamp that would be even more valuable – if it ever came on the market. That's the British Guiana 1c Magenta, which is regarded by many philatelists as the world's most famous stamp. Only one specimen is now known to exist, and when it last came on to the market – in 1980 – it fetched £600,000. Who knows what it would go for today!

A mistake on an otherwise ordinary stamp can greatly increase its value. For example, the American Inverted Jenny (also known as an Upside Down Jenny or Jenny Invert), a 1918 stamp in which the image of the aeroplane in the centre of the stamp was accidentally printed upside-down. It's probably the most

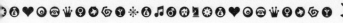

famous error in American stamps, and if
you chanced upon one, it would be worth
£500,000. Yes, half a million pounds just
because a bit of a stamp was printed the wrong
way round!

How did the search engine 'Google' get its name?

Google was founded by Larry Page and
Sergey Brin in 1996 while they were studying
at Stanford University, California. It wasn't
something they created in their spare time: it
was actually a research project.

Back then, conventional search engines ranked
results by counting how many times the search
terms appeared on the page. The Google Guys
(as they became known) thought there was
a better way of doing it: why not look at the
relationships between websites and work out
a website's relevance by the number of pages
and the importance of those pages. In other
words, they made sure that when you entered
a search term, you didn't get the websites

with the most times that the search term was mentioned: you got the sites that made the most sense to you, that was of the most value to you. And why? Because these were the sites, ranked in descending order of relevance, that all the previous people who had ever used your search terms had decided were the most useful to them.

In other words, you were benefiting from cumulative knowledge and usage.
Page and Brin originally nicknamed their new search engine 'BackRub' because the system checked backlinks to estimate the importance of a site.

Later, they changed the name to Google, a play on the word 'googol' which is the number one followed by one hundred zeros. They picked this to show that the search engine would provide large quantities of information for lots of people.

The domain name for Google was registered in 1997 and the company Google was launched the following year. At first, they were based in a friend's garage.

Right from the beginning, the company's mission statement was 'to organize the world's information and make it universally accessible and useful'. And that's just what Google does – which is why it's the most popular search engine in the world today with over a billion daily hits.

What's the hardest thing for a ventriloquist to say?

The original meaning of ventriloquism was to 'speak through the stomach' – from the Latin words 'venter' (stomach) and 'loqui' (speak). Although nowadays we think of ventriloquists as entertainers, they used to be conmen who would conjure up voices and claim they were spirits of the dead.

The modern puppet-on-the-knee entertainer started in the last century when The Great Lester (1878–1956) formed a 'partnership' with a hand-carved dummy called Frank Byron Jr.

Anyway, enough of the background, let me answer the question. The hardest letters are 'b', 'p' and 'm'. These are often replaced with 'v', 't', 'd' and 'n' spoken quickly. Bearing that in mind, it's been reckoned that the hardest phrase of all to say is: 'Who dared to put wet fruit-bat turd in our dead mummy's bed? Was that you, Verity?'

Go on, give it a go!

Why do we say 'I got it from the horse's mouth'?

You must have heard this expression. Perhaps you asked a friend how they knew a piece of information and they replied (perhaps tapping their nose as they said so – it's optional), 'Never you mind, I got it from the horse's mouth'. In other words, they got it from the very best source – the person at the centre of news in question.

Of course, this expression is most associated with horse racing where someone might confide in someone else that a certain horse is going to win. 'How good's your information?' the person might ask the tipster – only to be told that they got it from the horse's mouth. Now clearly this is impossible so, in practice, it means that they got it from the horse's trainer or the jockey: in other words, the closest person to the horse.

Interestingly, although this expression is (obviously) based on horses, it has nothing to do with betting. Instead, it's to do with the fact that you can tell a horse's age by examining its teeth. After all, a horse dealer might lie to you but you can always find out the truth 'from the horse's mouth'.

Are pineapples anything to do with apples?

No.

Excuse me, Mitch (says my editor) *your readers want a little more of an explanation than that.*

OK. No, they're not.

That's still not enough information, Mitch.

All right, no, they're not . . . honestly, they're not. They're absolutely nothing to do with apples.

Now you're being silly, Mitch.

All right then, Lauren (she's my editor – though she looks young enough to be one of my readers), here's some background. When the Spanish explorers went to South America and saw a pineapple for the first time, they thought it looked like a pine cone and so they called it 'Pina'. The English added 'apple' to associate it with juicy delicious fruits – and so the name became pineapple. The native Brazilian Tupi name is 'ananas' (meaning 'excellent fruit').

What is – or was – Hobson's choice?

Hobson's choice is no choice at all.

Thomas Hobson (1554–1631) was the owner of a livery stable in Cambridge who rented out horses to people. Bit like a car-hire firm today. Anyway, he had a strict rule that customers had to take the horse nearest the stable door. If they didn't like that horse, then that was tough.

So in as much as they had a choice, it was the choice of taking the horse offered to them or no horse at all. In other words, Hobson's choice: take it or leave it.

Who first thought of water skiing?

In 1922, Ralph Samuelson mastered water skiing at Lake Pepin, Minnesota, USA. In his earlier attempts, he had used two boards as skis and a clothesline as a rope and he was only able to last a few seconds, but he made successful refinements to the 'skis' and worked out that leaning backwards in the water with ski tips up and poking out of the water at the tip would lead to greater success.

Samuelson would go on to become the first water-ski racer, first to go over a jump ramp, first to slalom ski, and the first to put on a water-ski show.

In 1966, the American Water Ski Association formally acknowledged Samuelson as the first water skier ever.

Why are very young children called 'infants'?

The word 'infant' means 'unable to speak' – taken from the Latin words for 'not' and 'to speak'. Having said that, babies are really quick to learn language and from about 10 months, they begin to grasp words. However, as you will have noticed if you have a baby brother or sister, they'll only apply those words to the things that interest them most.

As a new father, I was of course absolutely thrilled when my baby son pointed at me and said 'Daddy' – or, rather, 'Dadda' – for the first time. I was less thrilled when I later saw him point at the dog and say 'Dadda' too.

My friend told me that rocks could have snot – just like humans. Was he making this up?

This was a question I received from a reader

who told me that he had four of my books and was therefore 'my biggest fan' (to which I was tempted to reply 'not until you've bought them all you're not!').

I have to say that I hadn't heard of 'rock snot' and so I checked the date to make sure it wasn't April 1 (I am incredibly gullible: so much so that when a friend told me that the word 'gullible' wasn't in the dictionary, I believed him!).

Well it wasn't April Fools' Day and so I looked into it and discovered that rock snot – or *Didymosphenia geminata* – to give it its scientific name – does exist.

Didymo (as it's known for short) is a single-celled, freshwater alga. While the individual cells are invisible to the naked eye, Didymo can form large colonies attached to rocks and plants smothering the bottoms of streams and rivers with a thick yellow/brown layer of growth. The massive blooms can form distinctive flowing 'rats tails' that turn white at their ends and look similar to tissue paper. In recent years, this once rare species has been expanding forming excessive growths covering miles.

Does it matter?

Yes it does, Didymo can harm freshwater fish, aquatic plants, and important aquatic insects. So rock snot is as annoying as human snot!

Is the Channel Tunnel the longest underwater tunnel in the world?

The Channel Tunnel is a magnificent piece of engineering that provides Britain (and Britons) with a car and rail link to continental Europe. If you haven't done the journey then I urge you and your family to do it because it really is extraordinary to get on a train in England and get off it in France.

But is it the longest such tunnel in the world? Well, the Channel Tunnel is 50.5 kilometres long, which, you'd have thought, would have made it the longest underwater road tunnel by far. But you'd have been wrong because, in fact, Japan has the world's longest underwater rail tunnel. The Seikan Tunnel is 53.85 kilometres long. It travels beneath the Tsugaru Strait – connecting the islands of Honshu and Hokkaido. Although it is the longest traffic (railway or road) tunnel in the world, faster and cheaper air travel has left the Seikan Tunnel relatively underused.

Is it true that Albert Einstein – perhaps the cleverest person who ever lived – didn't do very well at school?

For years now there's been this popular image of Albert Einstein being a total duffer at school. It's not true – as I'll explain in a moment – but you can see why people would want it to be true, can't you?

Imagine! The most important scientist of the past hundred years was a bit of a dunce – or, at the very least, a bit of a non-achiever at school!

People – me included – like the idea that someone can go from zero to hero. It's a good story – what a Hollywood film-maker might call 'a great narrative arc' – and so it appeals to us, especially if we too were under-achievers at school!

'Einstein and I were both useless at school

and he went on to come up with the theory of relativity (or something). Maybe I could do the same!'

Maybe not.

Because, apart from the fact that Einstein was the genuine article: a real-life genius, he was also an excellent student in his schooldays.

So where did this myth start? Was it just a case of wishful thinking?

No, there was more to it than that. It turns out that it was all the fault of a writer who, while researching Einstein's past, came across his school report cards. The pupils were graded from one to six for all their subjects. One was the best and six the worst and, not surprisingly, Einstein received lots of ones because he was such a good student.

The confusion arose because the year after Einstein left, the school reversed its grading system – making one the worst and six the best.

The writer/researcher didn't know that there had ever been a grading change and (wrongly) assumed that all of Einstein's scores of one meant that he hadn't done well at school. Doh!

How many people does a whale have to kill before it's a killer whale?

Because of their name, many people assume that killer whales kill people. In fact, that's not how they got their name. They were originally called 'whale killers' by sailors who witnessed them attacking larger species of whale. Over the years, 'whale killers' became known as 'killer whales'. Thankfully, they don't attack people, but they do sometimes kill other whales, hunting them in packs. For this reason, they are also known as the 'wolves of the sea'.

In golf, why is one under par known as a 'birdie'?

The term 'birdie' for one under par (i.e. getting the ball in the hole in one shot less than most other proper golfers would) comes from a hole played by three American golfers at the Atlantic City Country Club in 1899. One of the players' balls hit a bird in flight on his second shot and landed inches from the hole. He putted in his third shot on the par-4 hole and he and his friends decided that there should be a name for his achievement . . . and that name would be a birdie!

Why do triangular sandwiches taste better that rectangular ones?

First of all, do they? I think they do – and so, obviously, does the reader who sent in the question. And we're not alone as 72 per cent of Britons polled said that they too prefer triangular sandwiches. But why? According to the food scientist I consulted, 'they taste better because they encourage a smaller bite, releasing flavour molecules more effectively'.

Why do we say that someone is as 'fit as a fiddle' – why not 'fit as a guitar'?

This is one of those many sayings or expressions that has come to mean something completely different from its original meaning. Nowadays, this expression means that

someone is very healthy or well-exercised.
However, when it was first used, the word fit
meant 'suitable' (as in 'fit for a king'). So 'fit as
a fiddle' meant 'as suitable as a violin'.

Now that is obviously totally meaningless. So
here's what it really meant. Suitable or fine.
The fiddle comes in because it alliterates with
(i.e. has the same first letter as) fiddle and also
because a fiddle (or violin) was thought to
be an instrument that, in order to be played
properly, has to be absolutely right.

As the word fit came to mean 'healthy', the
expression took on a double meaning that
made it much more widespread.

So how are you?
I'm fit, thank you.
How fit?
As fit as a fiddle.
Sounds so much better than 'fit as a guitar',
don't you think?

Why do people – particularly kids – stick their tongues out when they're concentrating?

There are two reasons for this. Firstly, it's a reflex that all human beings have from birth. It's our primitive way of telling people (originally our parents) that we're absolutely full, we can't take any more: we're literally pushing food away with our tongues. So you can see how that primitive reflex might be useful when we're really concentrating as we're effectively saying 'I'm giving all my attention to this problem so please don't bother me with anything else.'

The other reason why we stick out our tongues is because so much of our brain's activity is devoted to controlling our tongues. Think about it. Your tongue is constantly moving, helping you to swallow and stopping you from choking. To help it do this, it's covered with densely packed receptors, which are connected to the brain's language centres so it frequently moves to help form word shapes as you think. All this is sending a huge amount of data to your brain. Sticking your tongue out reduces its movement and cuts down on all this stuff – which means that you can use your brain for other things, like concentrating on your work.

Why do we cross our fingers for luck?

The crossing of one's fingers for luck dates back to the time of the persecution of early Christians. Fearing for their safety if they openly crossed themselves in public, they did so furtively, with their fingers.

Where do all the banks put all the money? How does it all fit?

The short answer to this question is that it DOESN'T all fit! Have you any idea how much space – say – £40,000,000,000 in notes and coins would require? Apart from anything,

bank robbers would be lining up in their droves to get in and steal it all.

So, instead, what happens is that banks keep enough money on the premises to cover their daily business – mostly local shopkeepers paying in cash and customers withdrawing cash via ATM machines.

So this prompts the question: where do the banks keep all their billions of pounds?

The answer to this is they don't.
Er, what do you mean 'they don't'?
Just that, they simply don't have all that money.
Then who does?
That's just it: no one does.

Let me explain. Most financial transactions – certainly all the larger ones – aren't made in cash: they're done by transfer. At no point is money handed over so no money is actually needed. All that matters is that someone is keeping score of how much each individual, each company and – most importantly for the sake of this question – each bank has or is worth.

Here's an example of what I mean. Let's say that your grandparents sell their home for £250,000 and put the money in the bank. Their account will be credited with £250,000 from the buyer but at no stage has that money been physically transferred.

Of course, your grandparents could withdraw that money – perhaps to buy their grandchildren some fantastic presents (you wish) – but the banks work on the basis that not ALL their customers will want to withdraw ALL their money on the same day. That only tends to happen when there's panic in the air and there's a 'run' on the banks . . . in which case the bank might have to restrict the amount that customers can withdraw or even close down altogether.

Fortunately, that happens only very rarely and the system works on the basis of trust and confidence with the Government supporting the banks if necessary.

If we evolved from apes, why are there still apes? Why didn't they evolve like us?

This is to misunderstand evolution. The point about evolution is that some of a species evolve into other species while others remain the same and either continue (like apes) or simply die out (like the dodo).

Every life-form on this planet has evolved. Species that have died out, such as Neanderthals, have gone extinct because they either couldn't compete effectively with other species or adapt to changes in their environment.

Evolution simply means that a species changes over time. Apes (and monkeys) still exist because, over years and years of natural selection, they continue to be well adapted to their environment.

Actually, humans didn't evolve from apes, but share a common genetic ancestor with modern

apes. In other words, that we're not descendants of apes, but (very) distant cousins.

Either way, there's no reason why we shouldn't both carry on surviving and thriving.

Why is it considered unlucky to spill salt?

In Leonardo da Vinci's famous painting The Last Supper, a salt cellar near Judas Iscariot is knocked over. This is said to have started the superstition that spilt salt is unlucky.

... and why is an unimportant person described as being 'beneath' or 'below the salt'?

Salt used to be very expensive. At the dinner table, a salt container had an important position, next to the host, or the most senior person at the table. The closer you sat to the host, the closer you were to the salt. Less important people sitting at the far end were sometimes said to be 'below the salt.'

What does the 'best boy' often credited at the end of a film, actually do? And why do we never see a best girl?

The best boy is the nickname given to the chief assistant of the gaffer. The gaffer is in charge of all the lighting on the film set. A best boy can also be an assistant to the key grip – person in charge of filming equipment. In short, a best boy's job involves helping out with the technical side of a film's production. You won't see a 'best girl' in the credits because the term 'best boy' is used for both genders.

By the way, the name 'gaffer' came from the early days of film when light was controlled by the use of tarpaulins held in place with long poles called gaffs.

How useful is your computer's spell checker?

I only ask because someone sent me a
wonderful rhyme that really does destroy the
myth that a computer spell checker ensures
you avoid making any spelling mistakes.
Sure, it can help with tricky words, but far too
often, it allows the wrong words to creep into
your writing.

Just read this aloud and you'll see what I mean!

I halve a spelling checker,
It came with my pea see.
It plainly marks four my revue
Mistakes I dew knot sea.
Eye strike a key and type a word
And weight four it two say
Weather eye am wrong oar write
It shows me strait aweigh.
As soon as a mist ache is maid
It nose bee fore two long
And eye can put the era rite
Its rarely ever wrong.
I've scent this massage threw it,

And I'm shore your pleased too no
Its letter prefect in every weigh;
My checker tolled me sew.

Why do washing machines have windows?

Good question! There's nothing really to see and most of us would probably rather watch telly than our clothes going round and round.

In fact, it's only front-loading washing machines that have windows. Washing machines that are loaded from the top tend not to have windows.

There's no real reason why manufacturers first put windows in the front – other than because there had to be a door anyway and maybe they thought that the people who were using them in the launderette would enjoy watching the machine doing all the hard work!

The only other advantage of washing machine windows is so that you can see if, by mistake, you've loaded either the cat or some brightly coloured garment that hasn't got its dye well fixed. Either way, it's almost certainly too late to do anything about it.

What does the scouting song 'ging gang goolie' actually mean?

You know the song – you must do even if you're not a scout yourself.

Ging gang goolie goolie goolie goolie watcha,
Ging gang goo, ging gang goo.
Ging gang goolie goolie goolie goolie watcha,
Ging gang goo, ging gang goo.

Hayla, oh hayla shayla, hayla shayla, shayla, oh-ho,
Hayla, oh hayla shayla, hayla shayla, shayla, oh.
Shally wally, shally wally, shally wally, shally wally,
Oompah, oompah, oompah, oompah.

So what does it all mean?

Er, nothing . . . and that's deliberate!

Lord Baden-Powell, the man who founded the scouting movement, wanted a song that scouts from different countries could easily learn without struggling with a language barrier.

So he wrote a song in gibberish during the first World Scout Jamboree in 1920. The tune is based on an extract from Mozart's Symphony No. 1, composed when he was only eight. The words are pure Baden-Powell: pure gibberish!

Why do we throw confetti over a bride and groom at a wedding?

The throwing of confetti – tiny bits of paper – is a relatively recent development. Traditionally, it was rice – although you can see why confetti would seem more appropriate (not to say more hygienic!). And the reason why rice was thrown over newlyweds was because rice was a symbol of fertility. So it was hoped that the chucking of rice would bring the happy couple many children.

Failing that, they would at least have something to put in their larder.

N.B. I made up the bit about having something to put in their larder. That's just silly.

Why are competitive people said to be trying to 'keep up with the Joneses'?

You might have heard this expression. Perhaps your mum will point out that someone's just bought a new car and drop a hint that she'd like one too to which your dad will reply 'I'm sorry but no. We're not even going to try to keep up with the Joneses'.

I should point out that the new car purchaser is almost certainly not called Jones (though it is a popular surname!) but the idea of 'keeping up with Joneses' reflects on how competitive people can be – especially with their neighbours.

In fact, we get the phrase from an American comic strip from a hundred years ago which ran for 28 years and was adapted into books, films and even musical comedies. The 'Joneses' of the title were the neighbours of the comic strip's main characters and were spoken of but never 'seen'. The artist who devised it based it on his attempts to keep up with his own neighbours.

How deserted does land have to be before it's known as a desert?

It's nothing to do with being deserted! Deserts aren't determined by their population but by water.

The official definition of a desert is any land where more water evaporates than is acquired through rain.

In other words, if there is a net loss of water – due to a mixture of hot sun and lack of rain –

Which probably explains why deserts are
deserted . . .

N.B. You should never confuse deserts (dry
places with very few cinemas or restaurants)
with desserts (sweet stuff you eat after your
meal). Could lead to all sorts of problems –
especially in the Sahara and also in restaurants.

Why are lollipops so called?

Believe it or not but 'Lollipop' was originally the name of a racehorse.

Honestly! I mean, would I lie to you?

Although there were similar products that pre-date the lollipop, the sweet itself was definitely named after a horse.

An American man named George Smith started making large boiled sweets mounted on sticks in 1908. He named them after a racehorse of the time, Lolly Pop.

The first sweets that resemble what we call lollipops date to the Middle Ages, when the nobility would often eat boiled sugar with the aid of sticks or handles. And it's worth pointing out that the Roma people used to eat toffee apples sold on a stick. Intriguingly, the Romany words for 'red apple' are 'loli phaba'.

Close, but no lollipop.

Who invented Play-Doh?

Play-Doh, the world's most popular modelling clay, was invented by Joseph and Noah McVicker, brothers from Cincinnati, Ohio in the US in 1955. Their company (Kutol Chemicals) mainly manufactured a product called Cincy, a wallpaper cleaner, which wasn't selling well. Joe's sister-in-law, a nursery school teacher, gave him an idea. She had been complaining about the modelling clay her pupils were using at school. They found the traditional stuff much too heavy to manipulate and mould. So Joe took his Cincy, added some almond perfume to give it its distinctive scent and sent it to his sister-in-law.

It was immediately hugely popular. No more sticky hands either – so teachers loved it as did the children's parents. Soon word spread and the Cincinnati Board of Education was using it in all their elementary schools.

It wasn't until 1965 that the McVickers patented their wallpaper cleaner as Play-Doh. It soon became a top selling product.

A year later, they introduced a softer Play-Doh in primary colours. Children mixed these to make other colours, which inevitably ended up as brown.

The Play-Doh Fun Factory let children extrude the material into interesting shapes, making mock hair, colourful spaghetti and pretend ice cream.

In the 1980s, Play-Doh expanded its range to eight colours. Later versions sparkled with glitter, glowed in the dark, or smelled like shaving cream.

Play-Doh is sold in more than 75 countries around the world. If all the Play-Doh made since 1956 were extruded through the Fun Factory it would make a 'snake' that would wrap around the world more than three hundred times.

Why do we laugh?

Why indeed! After many scientific studies, the

answer seems to be that laughter is a social activity. Apparently, we laugh up to thirty times more when we are with other people than when we're on our own and most of this 'social laughter' has nothing to do with jokes. We laugh because other people are laughing: it helps to make us feel good about ourselves and it makes us part of the group – something essential to our survival as a species.

However, it's not something that we have much control over. Spontaneous laughter comes from the oldest part of the human brain, which means we find it almost impossible to start or stop it. In fact, human beings were able to laugh thousands of years before we were capable of speech.

Why is it always Dad who does the barbecue? . . . and why is it always Mum who has to clear it up?

It's true though. I don't know of any family where there's a mother and a father where it isn't the father who does the barbecuing. The same is true of my family – although nowadays it's my (elder) son who takes the tongs.

I think it goes back to our cavemen ancestors. There's something primeval about cooking meat over a fire that makes men feel like

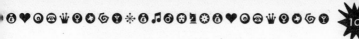
real men – even if the meat came from a supermarket rather than an animal they hunted that day.

But when it comes to barbecues, the fact that the man of the family will be in charge isn't the only certainty. Here are some others:

- **The more lighter fuel you use to get the barbecue going, the more likely you are to run out of matches.**

- The people who bring supermarket hamburgers always cook themselves steaks.

- **Any barbecue to which you invite more than six people will be washed out by rain.**

- The smoke from the barbecue can be guaranteed to waft into the garden of your least neighbourly neighbour.

- **The more gaudy the apron worn by the man doing the barbecue, the less likely it is that the meat will be cooked through properly.**

- It is impossible to toast hamburger buns on the barbecue without burning them.

- **The barbecue only really gets hot once all the food has been cooked.**

- If there aren't enough sausages to go around, the last one can always be guaranteed to fall on to the coals.

- **All other men attending will offer their (unwanted) advice on best barbecue techniques.**

Where's the remotest place on earth?

Antarctica, without a doubt. But if you move away from there (and you should, you know, as it's jolly cold), then the most remote place – certainly the most remote island – would be Tristan da Cunha. The nearest land mass is St Helena which is over a thousand miles away – and that's hardly a busy place itself!

Is there anything that children can do better than adults?

As an adult who can barely work his mobile telephone or do anything more than the most basic computer task, I would have thought that there were LOTS of things that children can do better than grown-ups.

Never mind the fact that they – you – have smaller fingers and so are physically better at handling fiddly tasks (like texting, which takes me at least twenty times longer than it takes the average child), it's obvious that children have a better mindset or mental capacity for modern life than their parents do.

Obviously, there are exceptions: adults who are absolute whizzes with technology and children who happen to have no interest in the subject but, by and large, I'd make that 1–Nil to the kids.

However, leaving those sorts of tasks to one side, are there any other areas in which you 'beat' us?

I mean, we're (on the whole) stronger and cleverer (at least in the sense that we know more).

We are, you know.

Oh no you're not!

Oh yes we are – and when did this book turn into a pantomime?

And yet there are areas in which children are definitely – and scientifically proven to be – 'better' than us adults.

For example, children dream more than adults do. And while we're on the subject of sleep, you are far more likely to sleepwalk than we are.

OK, so those aren't what you call 'accomplishments' but this one is: children can have better memory than adults. In one study, children were accurate 31 per cent of the time in identifying pictures of animals they had seen earlier, while adults were accurate only 7 per cent of the time.
Impressive, huh?

Also – and this is no mean feat – children are better at having fun and laughing.

You, as a child, might not value this ability to enjoy yourself, but many adults wish that they too could have fun as easily as children so obviously do.

But there's more!

Children can hear high frequency sounds that adults simply can't. We can't hear tones above 13,000 Hz. I guess that means that you kids are more like dogs than we are but, even so, it's another one to the kids.

And there's one more thing. Children are brilliant at squatting – especially when they're young. It's an important thing to be able to do and so many of us lose the ability to do it as we get older. We grown-ups sit or bend over – but we rarely squat.

Oh well, on balance, I'd say that the overall result is a draw. Children are as good as grown-ups.

Fair enough?

Is it true that Walt Disney's body was cryogenically frozen?

I've definitely heard this. Apparently – or so the story goes – when Walt died in 1966, his body was cryogenically frozen by being put into a

vat of liquid nitrogen so that when there was a cure to the cancer that killed him, he could be unfrozen, brought back to life and cured. If this story has echoes of the fairy tale of Sleeping Beauty then it's appropriate because this too is just that: a fairy tale.

When Walt Disney died he was cremated and his ashes were interred at the Forest Lawn Memorial Park in Glendale, California. So why did this rumour start?

I think there are a few reasons which all came together. Firstly, he was such an iconic figure in American culture that it was almost impossible to imagine him dying. Secondly, he himself was fascinated by scientific development. Now add in the fact that cryogenic freezing was very much in the news around the time of his death (the technology for it had just been invented and the first freezing would take place only a few weeks after his death) and you can see why people were so quick to believe it. However, if it's unsolved mysteries about Walt Disney you're after, consider this one. Apparently, the last thing he wrote before his death was the name of the actor Kurt Russell. Nothing more – just that: the name. Why? Who knows? Even Kurt Russell says he doesn't know!

Do the names of the days of the week actually mean anything?

Well they mean something to me! Saturday and Sunday are the days when I take time off work and relax while Monday is the day when . . .
(Stop it, Mitch, you know what the questioner means – Editor)
Oh all right, Lauren (my editor), I was only having a bit of a giggle.
(Well stop it right now – Editor)

People have always needed to distinguish the different days of the week (unless, I guess, they were on holiday and it didn't matter).

True, in times past, every day was exactly the same – apart from the Sabbath day of rest – but, even then, someone might need to arrange to meet someone else in a few days' time. So it made sense to give names to the days. And this is what people did.

We've inherited four of the names for our days from the Old English, two from the Norse and just one from the Romans.

Quite why it turned out that way is another question that is almost certainly impossible to answer.

Anyway, here are the days of the week and their origins.

Sunday is from the Old English sunnandaeg, meaning 'day of the sun'.
Monday is from the Old English monandaeg, or 'day of the moon'.
Tuesday is from the Old English tiwesdaeg, for the Norse god of combat, Tyr.
Wednesday is from wodnesdaeg, after the supreme Norse god Woden.
Thursday is from thorsdaeg, after the Norse god of thunder, Thor.
Friday is from frigedaeg, after Frigge, the Norse goddess of beauty, wife of Woden.
Saturday is named after Saturn, the Roman god of agriculture and the harvest.
It's interesting to compare and contrast the names of the days of the week in English and French. Whereas we have just one day named after a Roman God (Saturday), the French have several: they call Tuesday 'Mardi' (Mars's Day), Wednesday 'Mercredi' (Mercury's Day),

Thursday 'Jeudi' (Jupiter's Day) and Friday 'Vendredi' (Venus's Day).

As for Monday, we're all agreed that it's the day of the moon: we call it Monday and they call it Lundi (the French word for moon is lune).

Was the Barbie doll named after anyone?

She was! The Barbie doll started out as a real human being! She was Barbara Handler, the young daughter of businessmen Ruth and Elliot Handler.

In the early 1950s, Ruth Handler saw that her young daughter, Barbara, and her girlfriends enjoyed playing with adult female dolls as much or more than with baby dolls. Her mother realised that it was just as important for girls to imagine what they themselves might grow up to become as it was for them to focus on what caring for children might be like.

Unfortunately, the only adult dolls at the time

were made of paper or cardboard, Handler decided to create a three-dimensional adult female doll, one lifelike enough to serve as an inspiration for her daughter's dreams for her future. She then named it after her . . . now there's immortality!

The Barbie doll was launched at the American Toy Fair in New York City in 1959. Girls were desperate to own their own Barbie and the company sold 351,000 dolls in their first year and still couldn't meet customer demand. Since then, Barbie's popularity has rarely flagged; and today, with over one billion dolls sold, Barbie – together with her range of accessories – is the most successful doll in the history of the toy industry.

The first Barbie had a ponytail hairstyle, black and white zebra-striped bathing suit, open-toed shoes, sunglasses and earrings. A line of fashions and accessories was also available. Buyers at the industry's annual Toy Fair in New York were not impressed, but little girls certainly were and the Barbie doll took retailers by storm. Mattel, the manufacturer, was so swamped with orders that it took several years for supply to catch up with demand.

Although Barbie was originally a teenage fashion model, over the years that followed she took on many aspirational roles, such as doctor, dentist, firefighter, and even an astronaut.

How rare is a hole-in-one in golf?

Not that rare but some golfers go through their whole lives without ever achieving one. Basically, if an amateur player played golf every day, they could expect to hit an ace (as a hole-in-one is known) once every ten years.

Some golf tournaments – professional and amateur – offer special prizes, like a new car, for the first contestant to hit a hole-in-one. Usually such prizes are provided by sponsors, but sometimes the organizers of the tournament take out an insurance policy. The premium the organizers pay to an insurance

company is calculated on the basis of the odds against such an event occurring. According to insurance company actuaries (the people who make those calculations for the insurers), the odds against an average golfer making a hole-in-one at any given par three hole are about 12,500 to 1; whereas the odds against a professional golfer are a fifth of that: 2,500 to 1. This means that, at an amateur event, contested by a hundred people, the chances of someone – anyone – hitting a hole-in-one on one of the four par three holes are roughly 1 in 32.

In a professional tournament, the chances are even more likely that there will be a hole-in-one. Most PGA Tour events have 144 players. Therefore, the chances that there will be a hole-in-one during a single day of the tournament are about 1 in 4.5. Over the course of a standard four-day tournament – taking into account the fact that players are knocked out after two days – the odds are roughly 1 in 1 or 'evens'.

Could a (human) child ever be raised by animals?

This question goes all the way back to the legend of Romulus (the man who supposedly founded the city of Rome) and his twin, Remus, who were said to have been brought up by wolves when they were left to die.

Obviously that didn't happen – that's why they call it a 'legend' – but I was astonished to come across the following story in the course of my researches.

Read it and see what you think . . .

Nowadays, Rochom P'ngieng lives in a village in Cambodia, but she hasn't always lived there. When she was eight, she was tending buffalo near the Vietnam border when she vanished into the forest. No one knows precisely what happened to her, but it is thought she was seized by wolves. Instead of killing her, though, they raised her as one of them. So much so that after more than twenty years of living with these creatures, she prefers to crawl

rather than walk and is struggling to adapt to life among other people. Unable to speak any intelligible language, she can say only three words in the local language: mother, father and stomach ache. Her dad, who recognized her from a scar on her right arm when she was discovered, thought she had been eaten by a wild animal. So he was amazed to see her all those years later. She was found when local workers noticed that food had disappeared from a lunch box they left near a farm. They staked out the area and caught Rochom, who was naked with long hair down to her legs, trying to steal their rice.

'When I saw her,' he says, 'she was naked and walking in a bent forward position like a monkey. She was bare bones. She was shaking and picking up grains of rice from the ground to eat. When she is hungry, she pats her stomach as a signal. If she is not sleeping, she just sits and glances left and right, left and right.'

At first, Rochom refused to shower, wear clothes or use chopsticks. She would push her dad away and shout and cry, but eventually, she started cooperating. Her dad says, 'It is not easy, but life is waiting ahead for her'.

Meanwhile, her whole family are keeping a close eye on Rochom – called Wolf Woman by the villagers after she took off her clothes and acted as if she was going back into the jungle. The local chief of police says, 'Unfortunately, she keeps crying and wants to go back to the jungle. She is not used to living with humans.' Villagers from the Phnong hill tribe minority believe she is possessed by the evil spirits of the jungle and they brought in Buddhist monks to bless her.

Unfortunately, Rochom still isn't fully 'better'. She prefers to eat and live in a small chicken coop by her family's house, but she does at least join them for meals. And even if she still doesn't speak, she is at least starting to make eye contact.

Incredibly, this is not the only example I found of a child being 'raised' by animals.

Oxana Malaya was discovered living with wild dogs on a run-down farm in the Ukraine. She

ate raw meat and scraps and ran around on all
fours barking.

Apparently, when she was three, her extremely
neglectful parents left her outside one night and
so she crawled into a hovel where they kept
dogs. When no one came looking for her, she
stayed with the dogs and became one of them.
Eventually, five years later, a neighbour reported
it to the authorities and she was rescued.

So from the evidence of those two stories, it's
quite clear that human children can be 'raised'
by animals – but only at the cost of losing their
(for the want of a better word) 'humanity'.

Is it known who – if anyone – invented the tea bag?

The tea bag was invented by Thomas Sullivan
of New York in or around 1908. Sullivan, a
tea and coffee merchant, began packaging tea
samples in tiny silk bags, but many customers
brewed the tea in them. When he heard about
this, Sullivan saw a commercial opportunity

and started selling tea bags made of very thin paper.

Tea itself is said to have been discovered in 2737 BC by a Chinese emperor when some tea leaves accidentally blew into a pot of boiling water.

Do St Bernards still carry brandy to stranded mountaineers?

No they don't! In fact they never did: the little barrel of brandy was just a myth. What they did do was to go out in the snow after an avalanche to look for survivors. The dogs worked in male female pairs. Both would dig victims out. The female would lie next to them to keep them warm, while the male would go for help. St Bernards are named for the hospice at Great St Bernard Pass in the Swiss Alps that was run by Augustinian monks. One dog, named Barry, is famous for having saved more than forty people.

Why do round pizzas come in square boxes?

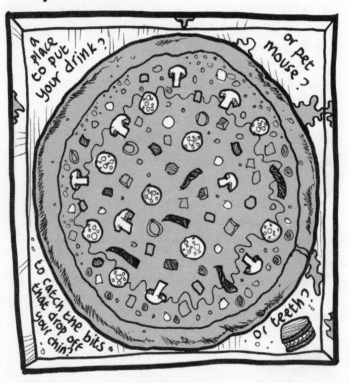

Good question: after all, isn't it a waste of cardboard? The corners could be cut off all those square boxes and used to make more boxes (square and round).

And it's not just pizzas but cakes too.

I decided to phone a friend of mine (well, he's the brother of a friend) who actually owns a factory that manufactures cardboard boxes just like those used for pizzas.

When I told him what I wanted to know he said, *'Oh no, not that old thing again'*.

What?
'People are always asking me that.'

Well, perhaps you might like to tell me and then those people who read my book will know and won't bother you again.

'Oh, all right. Look, Mitch, I run a business, OK. I make boxes. All sorts – from great big ones that people use for storage down to tiny ones for jewellery and things like that.
'When it comes to pizzas, it's a case of one size fits all.'

But pizzas come in different sizes.

'Yes of course they do but basically there are

*only a few different standard boxes and none
of them is round because it would cost more
to produce them for just one pizza shop. We'd
have to set up new machines and production
lines and the costs would be astronomical.'*

But, hang on, are you saying that if every
pizza place wanted round boxes it would be
possible?

He stopped to consider my point. *'I suppose
so but it's not a problem so why try to fix it.
They're happy, we're happy, the consumer is
happy . . .'*

But you're wasting cardboard.

'OK, so you're not happy.'

No, it's not that.

*'It's also a question of storage: square boxes
are easier to store and assemble. They come
flat, you know. It would be harder to do that
with round boxes. So we wouldn't be able to
transport as many of them in our lorries – or
we'd have to use more lorries. So what would*

you rather: that we use less cardboard or less petrol?'

Well, obviously, less petrol.

'Happy now?'

Blissfully.

Is it true that Roman emperors would spare the life of a defeated gladiator by giving him a thumbs up?

In Roman times, gladiators fought to the death. According to legend, when one gladiator was about to kill his opponent, he would look to the emperor who would either raise his thumb to spare the man, or lower his thumb to condemn him to death.

But it didn't happen like that. Thumbs weren't involved at all and were just (yet another)

Hollywood invention for the movies. However, the emperor could and did sometimes show mercy . . . and this is how it worked. When the winning gladiator looked up at the emperor, he would reply with an open or closed hand. If his hand was open – with a flat palm – then it meant 'spare his life' but if the emperor's hand was closed, it meant 'kill him'. If a gladiator killed his opponent before the emperor gave his permission, the gladiator would be put on trial for murder, as only the emperor had the right to condemn a man to death.

Why is Father Christmas also known as Santa Claus?

While we in Britain have Father Christmas, in other countries they have St Nicholas. The Dutch pronounce his name as Sint Klass or Sinter Klaas. When they emigrated to the US, they took their customs with them.

From Sinter Klaas, it's easy to see how Santa Claus entered our lives.

Did people really use to put animals on trial?

Incredibly, they did! As I explained in my *That's So Gross: Animals book* (available in all good bookshops, etc.), people used to think that justice had to be extended to animals as well as to people.

The trial and punishment of animals was especially common in France. The reason why pigs were so often on trial is because in the Middle Ages, they were allowed to wander freely around French villages – sometimes with disastrous consequences.

Here are some examples that weren't in *That's So Gross: Animals:*

1463: In Amiens, France, two pigs were sentenced to be buried alive because they had 'torn and eaten with their teeth a little child . . . who for this cause passed from life to death'.

1497: In Charonne, France, a sow ate the chin of a child. The court condemned the sow to death – by a blow on the head. So far, so fair, but they didn't stop there. They ordered that the sow's flesh be cut into pieces and fed to dogs, and that the sow's owner and his wife go 'on a pilgrimage to Notre-Dame of Pontoise on the day of Pentecost'.

1499: In Cauroy, France, a bull was condemned to be hanged for 'having furiously killed a boy of fourteen or fifteen'.

1557: In the Commune of Saint-Quentin, France, a pig was condemned to be 'buried all alive . . . for having devoured a little child'.

1796: Beutelsbach, Württemberg, Germany. The town bull was buried alive after disease had killed many cattle. It's not certain whether this was intended as punishment for infecting cattle or, more probably, as a kind of ritual sacrifice. Interestingly though, it wasn't done by simple peasants on the spur of the moment, but by a vet on official orders and it was done in public in front of a large crowd.

Why are baked beans always sold in tomato sauce?

I guess because that's the way people like 'em! They weren't always: until 1895, people ate them without any particular sauce or just with butter. People also ate them for the most peculiar of reasons: in the 17th century people consumed them because they thought they cured baldness.

Then, in 1895, Henry J. Heinz (yes, that Heinz) created baked beans in tomato sauce in Pittsburgh, USA. They were introduced to Britain nine years later where they were sold with a lump of pork and considered a great delicacy.

Once British factories started making them, they came down in price and proved to be incredibly popular. So much so that more baked beans are sold in the UK than anywhere else. The slogan 'Beanz Meanz Heinz' was used for more than 22 years to advertise the product.

How can I tell if my pet rabbit is happy or not?

You can tell how a rabbit is feeling by looking at the position of its ears. If the ears are standing tall, pointing forward, the rabbit is happy and curious. If the ears are laid completely flat on its back and are pointing backwards, the rabbit is annoyed or frightened.

Who is the 'fair lady' in the nursery rhyme 'London Bridge is Falling Down'?

London Bridge is falling down,
Falling down, falling down.
London Bridge is falling down,
My fair lady.

'London Bridge is Falling Down' is a well-known nursery rhyme and, like many such songs, has its roots in history.

There are two possible candidates for the 'fair lady'. It's either Matilda of Scotland (c. 1080–1118), the wife of King Henry I, who was responsible for the building of a series of London bridges, or Eleanor of Provence (c.1223–1291), the wife of King Henry III who had custody of the bridge income from 1269 to 1281.

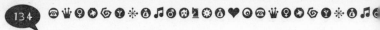

Why does the prime minister have a 'cabinet'?

Every Prime Minister has a cabinet consisting of the most important members of his Government – including such key people as the Chancellor of the Exchequer, the Home Secretary and the Foreign Secretary. In other words, the cabinet helps the Prime Minister to govern the country.

But why is this group called a cabinet? After all, isn't a cabinet just a place where you keep things? We have a bathroom cabinet in which we keep toothpaste and tablets for when we have headaches – how on earth did such a word come to be used for a Prime Minister's colleagues.

In fact, this goes back to the days before Prime Ministers when the king (or queen) governed the country. Monarchs needed advisers too, and they used to meet with them in small private rooms called 'cabinets' to discuss matters of state. From this word, we get the modern cabinet.

What's the longest road in the world?

Off the top of my head, I'd say any road on which you're travelling with young kids in the back intermittently throwing up and asking 'how long till we get there?'

But then I'm speaking as a dad and not as The Man Who Knows Everything (or-is-supposed-to-but-usually-gets-caught-out).

So let me tell you that the world's longest international highway or motorway is the Pan-American Highway, which connects many countries in the Americas. It's just under 48,000 kilometres long

The longest national highway within a single country is Australia's Highway 1, which is over 20,000 kilometres long and runs almost the entire way around the country's coastline. It links nearly all the country's major coastal cities (although Brisbane and Darwin are not directly connected, and the capital, Canberra, is inland). The world's widest highway or motorway is the Katy Freeway (part of Interstate 10) in Houston, Texas. Some sections have up to 26 lanes – although some of these lanes are restricted for use by different categories of driver or vehicle.

So, which famous person was born on the same day as you?

Note I said 'day' and not 'date' which means that approximately one-seventh of the whole world's population was born on the same day as you!

You've probably heard the old rhyme:

Monday's child is fair of face,
Tuesday's child is full of grace,
Wednesday's child is full of woe,
Thursday's child has far to go,
Friday's child is loving and giving,
Saturday's child works hard for a living,
But the child born on a Sabbath day
Is bonny and blithe, and good and gay.

Does that apply to the day on which YOU were born?

According to that, your whole personality is based on the day of the week on which you happened to be born.

As if!

But it's certainly a fun game to play!

By going to the site
http://www.maxxmktg.com/birthday.html

I was able to discover that I was born on a
Monday – making me 'fair of face' . . . and
who could possibly argue with that (silence at
the back, there!).

Anyway, once you've found out your day of
birth (alternatively, you could ask your mum:
believe me, she'll remember), take a look at
the lists below and see just some of the famous
people who share your day.

MONDAY
Denise Van Outen, British TV presenter
Leonardo DiCaprio, American actor
Katie Holmes, American actress
Lewis Hamilton, British motor racing driver
Prince William, British royal

TUESDAY
Tiger Woods, American golfer

Keira Knightley, British actress
Cristiano Ronaldo, Portuguese footballer
Ashton Kutcher, American actor
Jennifer Aniston, American actress

WEDNESDAY
Sir Alex Ferguson, British football manager
Britney Spears, American singer
Victoria Beckham, British singer
Will Smith, American actor

THURSDAY
Theo Walcott, British footballer
Sir Paul McCartney, British singer/songwriter
Declan Donnelly (as in Ant & Dec), British
entertainer
Harry Hill, British comedian
Wayne Rooney, British footballer
Jonathan Ross, British TV presenter

FRIDAY
David Beckham, British footballer
Princess Eugenie, British royal
Mariah Carey, American singer
Steven Gerrard, British footballer
David Walliams, British actor and comedian

SATURDAY
Madonna, American singer and actress
Daniel Craig, British actor
Kate Middleton, Duchess of Cambridge
Dame J.K. Rowling, British writer
Colin Firth, British actor

SUNDAY
Emma Watson, British actress
Phillip Schofield, British actor and TV presenter
Johnny Depp, American actor
Ricky Gervais, British actor and comic
Daniel Radcliffe, British actor

Is it true that word 'news' is an acronym for 'north, east, west, south'?

It's a nice thought, isn't it? After all, the news is gathered from all four corners of the world so why shouldn't it derive its name from those four corners?

Unfortunately, this is almost certainly one of

those explanations that occurred to people after the word had already been invented.

Quite simply, the word 'news' is the plural of the word 'new'. In other words, the news consists of new things that are happening. It was only later that people said, 'hey, hang on a minute' – or words to that effect – 'these are the first four letters of the four main points of the compass: it must explain the use of the word "news".'

Who invented fuzzy felt?

Fuzzy Felt is an entirely British invention, developed by a Buckinghamshire woman named Lois Allan. During the Second World War, Lois offered the use of her outhouses to the government for the manufacture of felt gaskets and filter-disks for armoured tanks.

Many of the women who came in to work in the factory had small children who were getting in the way of the machinery. Lois had studied fashion in Paris in the 1920s and, using her art training, had the brilliant idea of collecting up the off-cuts of felt from the gasket-making and turning them into shapes to amuse the children. Using her dining-room table-mats turned upside down, she found that the felt stuck to the cork base.

After the war ended, Lois and her husband realised that the fuzzy felt could be developed commercially. They set up Allan Industries in 1950, continuing to employ many of the women who had made the gaskets and filter disks – and sold their toy. The first sets cost about 35p (in today's money).

Part of the appeal of Fuzzy Felt for people who didn't have much money following the War was the fact that it was reusable. Also it was simple and could be played with anywhere, at any time. Lois continued to design all the Fuzzy Felt products, which included farmyard animals and Bible stories – the latter being a very big commercial success in America.

Among the most popular were the ballet and horses sets, which are sadly no longer in production, but many may have been

tucked away in attics along with sets featuring Winnie the Pooh, Noddy, circuses, jungles and hospitals.

Over 25 million sets have been sold since it began. Stretched end to end, they would reach as far as the moon and back.

Whose idea was it to sell fish fingers?

We have to thank Clarence Birdseye for the fish finger. He was an American inventor who noticed food that had been frozen tasted just as good as it had when it was fresh. He decided to open factories processing frozen fish and eventually sold his business to a company that changed its name in his honour to Birds Eye.

The fish finger was invented to help British fishermen find larger markets for their increasingly large catches of cod. The first fish fingers were made in the Birds Eye factory in Great Yarmouth in 1955. They did experiment with herrings as well but in blind tastings most people preferred the cod fingers.

The advertising campaign was 'no bones, no waste, no smell, no fuss'. These days we get through more than 1.5 million Birds Eye fish fingers every day. In 2009, the artist Banksy featured the fish finger as part of his art exhibition in Bristol. The fish fingers were 'swimming' around in a fish bowl.

What would happen to an astronaut if they fell into outer space? Would they explode?

According to all the (inevitably low budget) films I've ever seen, they do just that: they explode or, at the very least, pop.

In fact this is just yet another example of Hollywood distorting reality for the sake of drama. In fact, a person who fell into outer space without their helmet and oxygen supply

would simply lose consciousness and then die.

Could they survive at all?

Well, yes, but only for a few seconds and only then so long as they remembered to breathe out before going into outer space.

Who invented crisps?

The crisp – or, as the Americans call it, the potato chip – was created in Saratoga Springs, New York on 24 August 1853.

Annoyed by a diner who kept sending his fried potatoes back because they were too thick and bland, a hotel chef named George Crum decided to slice the potatoes as thinly as possible, frying them until crisp and seasoning them with extra salt.

Crum was intending to insult his customer with these ultra-thin fried potatoes, but instead he ended up pleasing him and they soon became a regular item on the hotel's menu under the name 'Saratoga Chips'.

In the 20th century, crisps spread beyond restaurants and began to be mass-produced as snacks with flavours being added later.

Why do mosquito bites itch?

The reason most mosquito bites itch is because mosquitoes inject saliva into the person's skin before they suck your blood. They take it out once they are done, but if they are forced to fly away, they don't get a chance to draw the saliva out. And it is their saliva that causes the itch.

Has an animal ever been fitted with glasses?

Don't be silly. Of course they haven't – except as a joke for a photo. It's hard enough for us humans to keep glasses on our heads so how would you persuade an animal to wear a pair? However, that's not to say that animals don't suffer from bad eyesight. Many animals have their (short) lives blighted by poor vision and so the lucky ones are fitted with contact lenses. No, I'm not kidding! Think about it: contact lenses are a much better solution than glasses as most animals can't touch their eyes to remove them whereas they'd simply shake off their specs.

In fact, it was a German company, S & V Technologies, that developed contact lenses for animals, including lions, giraffes, tigers and bears suffering from cataracts.

According to the head of the company's veterinary division, 'Cataracts generally means blindness for animals, unlike for humans, and because animals have short lifespans, it means

losing quality of life in a greater share of that life.'

Since its launch in 2008, the firm has helped a sea lion at a water park who had trouble performing his tricks due to severely blurry vision, a blind kangaroo in an Australian nature park and a visually impaired lioness in a Romanian zoo.

The company also came up with a solution to help horses afflicted with 'head shaker syndrome': special lenses that absorb UV rays. Of course, such treatment is costly and so these lenses are only fitted to extremely valuable breeding or racing horses.

Why is the room where people relax when they're making TV programmes called a green room?

As you know, many – if not most – of my

questions come from my readers, but this is one I posed for myself because I've always wanted to know the answer.

Having worked in television – as a researcher, director, producer and performer, I have been ushered into many green rooms – none of which were actually green – and often wondered how this area of relaxation for performers and crew got its name.

According to some sources, at the turn of the 17th century, London's Blackfriars Theatre had a room behind the scenes where the actors waited to go on stage and because it was painted green, it was called 'the green room'. When other theatres – and, later, television studios – had similar rooms they too were named 'green rooms'.

Another possibility is that 'green room' might be a corruption of 'scene room', the room where scenery was stored which doubled as the actors' waiting/warm-up room.

I don't like that explanation as I think it's too far-fetched. Instead, I prefer the idea that the room is green because that's the colour nervous – and therefore nauseous – actors go before a perfomance.

A couple more possibilities before I tell you a wonderful story. In 18th-century theatre, the main actors waited for their entrances in the wings – i.e. at the sides of the stage – whereas the minor inexperienced actors were banished behind the scenes. Another word for inexperienced is 'green'. You can work it out from there.

Finally, the most plausible suggestion is that in English theatres, a green floor-cloth was traditionally spread on the stage for tragedies. During the Restoration, when virtually all performances were comedies, the green floor-cloth for tragedies was stored in the actors' waiting room and used to deaden their footsteps so the sound of actors walking around wouldn't disturb the performance. As tragedies were rarely performed, the green floor-cloth became a routine fixture of the actors' lounge and the room became known as the green room.

As I often write in situations where there are so many possibilities, it's your choice. My own instinct is that it's a mixture of many of the above – coupled with the fact that green is a soothing and restful colour.

At this point, I must tell you a story about a place I used to work called the Greenwood Theatre. It was a fine auditorium attached to Guy's Hospital where many TV programmes were made. It also had an excellent green room which served delicious food, but that's not why I'm telling you about it. No, my story is about the theatre itself, which was named after the man – Greenwood – who endowed it (i.e. left money in his will for it to be built). According to legend, he intended for an operating theatre to be built but, by mistake, an acting theatre was constructed instead. Apparently, his surviving relatives were furious when they found out but, by then, it was too late to change it.

As I say, I don't know if it's true but I so want it to be!

Why is there a silent 'b' in words like 'lamb' and 'doubt'?

This perfectly sensible question has a really silly answer.
It's because scholars wanted to show off their knowledge!

By the 15th century, most English words had their origins in either Anglo-Saxon or French (after the Norman Invasion of 1066). It was at this point that scholars decided to have their say. The word 'doubt', for example, was then spelt 'dout'. Nothing wrong with that, you'd think, as it had come from the French word 'doute'.

Aha,' said the scholars who wanted to revive the classical world of the Greeks and the Romans, 'this word has its origins in Latin, It comes from the word 'dubitare'. Let's add a 'b' to reflect that (and to show how jolly clever we are!)'

And that's what they did, reader. Dout became doubt and other words suffered the same fate. So much so that our language is now haunted by silent letters.

The d is always silent in words like adjective and adjacent.
The g is always silent in words like gnarl and sign.
The h is always silent in words like ghost and ghastly.

The k is always silent in words like knee and knowledge.

Makes spelling tests fun though, doesn't it?

Was Marie Antoinette being mean when, during the French Revolution after being told that the starving people had no bread, she said 'Let them eat cake'?

According to popular myth, Queen Marie Antoinette was supposed to have said (about the poor people of Paris): 'S'ils n'ont plus de pain, qu'ils mangent de la brioche.' ('If they have no bread, let them eat brioche').

This has travelled down the ages as 'let them eat cake' – a lofty dismissive thing to say to poor people. It would be as if a rich person today heard about people struggling to afford

mince said, 'Well why don't they eat steak?'
Based on this quotation, Marie Antoinette,
the wife of King Louis XVI who was deposed
in the French Revolution of 1789, has had a
posthumous (that's to say 'post-life') reputation
as a heartless woman who was out of touch
with her people and therefore deserved her
fate – death by the guillotine.

Well, she didn't say any such thing! Those precise words were actually written years earlier by the writer and philosopher, Jean-Jacques Rousseau, in his book *Confessions* in which he wrote 'I recalled the make-shift of a great princess who was told that the peasants had no bread and who replied: "Let them eat brioche".'

So attributing the words to Marie Antoinette was probably just revolutionary propaganda that happened to stick.

However, there's a twist! It turns out that even if she had said those words – and she didn't – then they wouldn't necessarily have been stupid or unfeeling.

Let me explain. The law at the time she and her husband reigned was that bakers who ran out of ordinary bread, had to sell their finer bread (such as brioche) at the same price as the cheaper bread. This law was to protect poorer people from ruthless bakers who would make insufficient quantities of cheap bread so that they only had expensive bread left, which would earn them much more money.

So the comment 'let them eat brioche' would actually have been a perfectly reasonable response!

Why do people say 'I'll take a raincheck' when they decide to do something later instead of now?

You'd think it would mean that they would see what the weather is doing later before deciding on their plans and, I suppose, that's what this phrase has come to mean but the origins are slightly different.

In the US, a raincheck was offered to people who had tickets to a baseball game that was rained off. They would be given a raincheck, which was a ticket for a game at a later date. So actually a raincheck is a substitute for something you want rather than a decision to put something off for the future but you can see how the expression evolved!

Why do gorillas beat their chests?

No, it's not (as I thought) because they're showing off. Gorillas beat their chests when they get nervous.

So what have hyenas got to laugh about?

Is there some joke that they're in on that the rest of us –the whole animal kingdom – know absolutely nothing about?

Er, no. The hyena's laugh – actually more of a high-pitched cackle – isn't like a human laugh. While we laugh (mostly) because we've found something funny or (sometimes) out of nervousness or embarrassment, the hyena laughs as a means of communication. Zoologists who have studied them say that the hyena's laugh carries important information to both friends and enemies and also helps to establish the hyena's place in the hierarchy.

Has anyone ever swum from one continent to another?

The shortest distance between two continents is across the Strait of Gibraltar, which divides Europe from Africa. Although, at their closest, the two continents are just 12 kilometres, less than eight miles, apart, the routes most swimmers usually take are longer because of the currents.

More than 200 people have swum one way across one of the world's busiest shipping channels. Five people have swum both ways (i.e. there and back).

So although it sounds more impressive to have swum between two continents (rather than between two countries), it is far harder to swim across the even busier English Channel which is twice as far and a lot, lot colder!

Which is my cue to heap a whole lot of praise on David Walliams who has swum the Strait of Gibraltar, the English Channel and the entire length of the River Thames. What a hero!

Why is the army rank of colonel pronounced 'kernel'?

After all, it looks like it should be pronounced 'co-lo-nel'.

As you know, a colonel is a senior officer in the army. The word comes from the Old Italian word 'colonello' (meaning commander of troops, which in turn derived from the Italian word for 'column').

Like so many words, the word came into English through the French. However – and this is where it gets more complicated – it came through as two separate words: colonel and coronel.

The word 'coronel' was eventually pronounced as 'kernel'.

The someone decided that the word should be spelled the way it was originally and so it should be colonel.

Are you still with me?

I could understand if you weren't because I'm having trouble with it and am almost losing the will to live.

Anyway, the word was now spelt as 'colonel' but still pronounced as 'coronel' or 'kernel'. So now you know.

Why do chefs wear those tall hats?

A chef's hat is shaped the way it is to allow air

to circulate around the scalp, keeping the head cool in a hot kitchen.

THE REAL REASON WHY, CHEF'S HATS ARE SO TALL.

Why is someone's favourite person said to be 'the apple of their eye'?

This phrase comes from the Bible. Psalm 17:8 asks God (to) 'keep me as the apple of your eye'. So being the apple of someone's eye would be a good thing – even if an apple in the eye would ruin all vision. Or is that the point?

Were there two people named Häagen and Dazs who got together to make the ice-cream company?

What, you mean like Ben & Jerry?

Er, no. There wasn't even a single person with either of those names.

So why is it called Häagen-Dazs?

To answer that question, I must tell you a little of the history of the company.

It all started with Reuben and Rose Mattus, two Polish immigrants to the US, in 1961.

They created the ice-creams (just three flavours, chocolate, vanilla and coffee, to start with) and they decided to give their product a foreign-sounding name that might impress the American public. This is known in the marketing industry as foreign branding. Reuben thought that because Denmark was known for its dairy products and had a positive image in the US, it might be an idea to give his company a Danish sounding name and, in fact, he included an outline map of Denmark on early labels.

But, ultimately, as his daughter Doris once revealed, he just wanted a name that would stand out as unique and totally original – which is why he would sit at the kitchen table for hours saying nonsensical words until he came up with a combination he liked.

Why do the americans call autumn 'Fall'?

I always thought it was because the Americans, being simpler than us Brits, were more literal. "Look," they'd say to one another as the trees shed their leaves, "fall!". Whereas we Brits, being more sophisticated, had a proper word for the season.

After all, we don't call winter 'cold' or summer 'hot' – so why call autumn 'fall'?

Well, once again I'm forced to apologise to my American friends because it turns out that they're right and we're wrong!

From the late 17th century, fall was the word for the third season of the year used by people on both sides of the Atlantic. It wasn't until the 18th century that we Brits began to use the 14th century word 'autumn' which was derived from the French while the Americans continued to use fall.

Why do people call fingers 'pinkies'?

Like Santa Claus, this is another word/ expression we get from the Dutch who have a word that means 'little finger'. And that word is? Yup, you guessed it 'pinkie'.

Why do we cock our heads when we're confused or are having difficulty understanding something?

Humans - and animals - cock their heads when confused to help both sight and hearing. What we're doing is changing the way we see and hear things by moving our heads in to a different position. If it's very important, we might even move our bodies as well, but generally it's enough just to move – or – cock our heads to capture sights and sounds in a different plane.

Is there any meaning to the gifts given by 'my true love' in the carol, *The Twelve Days of Christmas?*

Yes there is!

A partridge in a pear tree represents Jesus Christ, son of God

Two turtle doves = the old and new Testaments

Three French hens = the Theological Virtues of faith, hope, and charity

Four calling birds = the four gospels

Five gold rings = the first five books of the Old Testament (also known as the Pentateuch)

Six geese a-laying = the six days that God took to create the universe

Seven swans a-swimming = the seven gifts of the Holy Spirit, the seven sacraments

Eight maids a-milking = the eight Beatitudes

Nine ladies dancing = The nine fruits of the Holy Spirit

Ten lords a-leaping = The ten commandments

Eleven pipers piping = The eleven faithful apostles

Twelve drummers drumming = The twelve points of doctrine in the Apostle's Creed

Is there any connection between a punch in boxing and the fruit-based drink of the same name?

Alas, none whatsoever! The drink punch derives from from the Hindi word 'panch' meaning five as the drink was made from five different ingredients: spirits, sugar, lemon juice, water, and spices. There is an alternative explanation – that it may have derived from a puncheon, a cask holding 72 gallons, from which a punch bowl could be made. But the former is much more likely

A boxing punch, on the other hand, originally (in the 14th century) came from the word 'pounce' – meaning 'swoop' or 'lunge'. But it has nothing to do with the drink – unless you believe that someone who's drunk too much alcohol is more likely to punch people!

How exactly is decaffeinated coffee de-caffeinated?

Caffeine is the naturally-occurring chemical in coffee that's responsible for the 'hit' (i.e. the mild stimulatory effect on the central nervous system). A standard cup of coffee typically contains about fifty milligrams of caffeine – although the amount varies considerably depending on the method of preparation and the blend of coffee

Personally, I can't tell the difference between

caffeinated and decaffeinated but, for people who are sensitive to caffeine, even five milligrams can be too much and that's why there's a huge market for decaffeinated coffee. In fact, one in every eight cups of coffee bought or sold is decaffeinated.

But, to return to the question, how is the caffeine removed to make coffee decaffeinated?

There are a few different techniques but the most common is to first soften the beans in water.

However, water, on its own, won't remove the caffeine – well, at least not without taking away all the flavour at the same time – so they use a stronger solvent than that. The most widely used solvent today is ethyl acetate, a compound found in many fruits.

And what happens to all the caffeine that is extracted? It's not thrown away but is sold off to soft drinks' companies who want to add caffeine to their products.

While we're on the subject of caffeine in coffee, office practical jokers have been known to switch the decaffeinated and regular coffees so that decaffeinated coffee drinkers get a surprising hit while caffeine addicts get increasingly tetchy without their regular fix.

That's very naughty indeed!

Why do cats rub against our legs?

I have to admit that I'm not a cat lover and I've always thought that cats can pick up on this and rub themselves against me as if to say, "Hah, I know you don't like me but I don't care!"

In fact, I wasn't that far off the mark. When a cat rubs up against you, it marks you with its scent in an attempt to claim ownership of you.

Give me dogs any day of the week!

Why do car owners allow their cars to be trashed in a demolition derby?

I've been to a demolition derby and jolly good fun it was too but I'm not sure it was what you or I would call a 'sport': it was more like lawless mayhem. Although they're held in the UK, they are more associated with the US. Basically a demolition derby consists of a whole bunch of battered old cars bashing into each other until only one car is left standing – or, at least, running. Honestly, I'm not making it up! The drivers deliberately ram their cars into each other. It's quite a spectacle. It's not just mindless anarchy though: there's actually a good reason for it. At our local racetrack, cars race in all different classes - a bit like Formula 1 but slower – and, at the end of the afternoon, there are inevitably quite a few battered cars that aren't worth patching up. So why not make an attraction out of a necessity?

What's the cheekiest thing anyone's ever done?

There's an urban legend – that's to say a story that people pass around that is probably untrue – that a lawyer from Charlotte, North Carolina, bought a box of very expensive cigars, then insured them against fire. Within a month, having smoked every single one of them – and despite the fact that he hadn't yet paid his first premium – the lawyer filed a claim, declaring that the cigars had been lost 'in a series of small fires'. The insurance company refused to pay, for the obvious reason: the man had merely consumed the cigars correctly. Nevertheless, the lawyer took them to court and won.

In handing out his ruling, the judge agreed with the insurance company that the claim was frivolous, but stated that the lawyer held a policy from the company in which it had warranted that the cigars were insurable and also guaranteed that it would insure them against fire. It had not defined what was considered to be unacceptable fire, and

therefore was obliged to pay the claim. The insurance company paid $15,000 to the lawyer for the loss of his cigars in the 'fires'.

After the lawyer cashed the cheque, however, the insurance company had him arrested on 24 counts of arson. With his own insurance claim used against him, the lawyer was convicted of intentionally burning his insured property and sentenced to 24 months in jail and a $24,000 fine.

Like I say, this is an urban legend and almost certainly NOT true but it's certainly an example of extreme cheek!

Are Brussels sprouts from Belgium?

Brussels is, of course, the capital of Belgium, so you'd think that the sprout – the mini-cabbage-like vegetable so popular (but not, I can assure you, with me) at Christmas – would have come from there.

You'd think that but you would be wrong.

Although they were grown in Belgium as long ago as the 13th century – which is how they got their name – they (or something very similar to them) were originally cultivated in ancient Rome.

In fact, if they were going to be called anything other than Roman Sprouts, they should probably be called Dutch Sprouts or (after the capital of The Netherlands) Hague Sprouts because that's where they're most popular. In fact, the Dutch grow 82,000 metric tonnes of the ghastly vegetables every year.
Yeuggh.

And they make you fart.

Why do bruises change colour?

You get a bruise after you've bumped yourself or someone – inevitably a brother or sister – has hit you. The bruise appears when the blood vessels under the skin are broken and, as a result, some blood leaks out. These are red blood cells, which turn the surface of the skin purple, but your white blood cells rush in to repair the damage. These break down the red blood cells and the first waste product is biliverdin, which is green. Chemicals in the body then convert this into waste matter called bilirubin, which is yellow. Bilirubin is taken to the liver to be excreted from the body. And while all this is going on, the original bruise changes colour from purple, to green to yellow and eventually fades away.

How did people keep food fresh before refrigerators were invented?

It was tricky – and so people tried their best to use foods or drinks that didn't need refrigerating or cooling. Wealthy people had icehouses, well insulated brick rooms often built underground, which were packed with snow or ice from ponds and lakes in the winter, in the hope it would stay frozen until

the next winter. Of course this ice was only good for keeping things cold, you couldn't use it for actual eating.

From the mid-19th century, the icebox – the forerunner of the refrigerator – helped improve (and change) the lives of ordinary people. Iceboxes were housed in wooden boxes – some of which could be really ornate and beautiful. They had hollow walls that were lined with tin or zinc and packed with various insulating materials such as cork, sawdust, straw or seaweed. A large block of ice was held in a tray or compartment near the top of the box. Cold air circulated down and around storage compartments in the lower section.

One drawback with iceboxes is that they required frequent visits from the iceman to replace the melted ice with fresh ice. In fact, in the days before refrigeration, the iceman was as common a sight as the milkman.

The first domestic refrigerator was General Electric's Monitor-Top, which was launched in 1927 (its name was based on its supposed resemblance to the gun turret on the 19th

century American warship Monitor). Over
a million of these fridges were produced,
although they weren't particularly safe because
of the chemicals they used.

From there, however, better, cleaner and safer
fridges were developed so that today, less than
a century on, there are very few homes indeed
that don't have a fridge.

Is it true that we use just a tiny proportion of our brains?

Well you might, but I use all of mine *(He has
to – Editor)*. No, stop it – it's true and it's not just
me: we all use all of our brains.

So why do people believe that we only use a
tiny proportion?

That's harder to answer. Firstly, it's true that many
people believe that we only use a small part of
our brains. They are wrong.

The brain has many different parts to it, which
are needed for different functions. For example,

we need the cerebellum for balance.
We need the hindbrain to control things like
breathing and heart rate. Basically, the brain
does a lot more than just think.

I suppose that's where the confusion arose: the fact that we don't use all of our brain just for thinking led some people to (wrongly) believe that we weren't using all of our brains. But we were – and we are!

I think also that some people – particularly so-called psychics (they're all frauds, you know) – rather liked the idea that there were 'unused' parts of the brain that they (and only they) could access. To spread mystery and confusion helps them peddle their stupid ideas.

But they're wrong. We all use all our brains – after all, why else would we have brains? It's just that some of us use them better than others *(Not you, Mitch – Editor)*.

How do trick birthday candles work?

You know what I mean! Those trick candles, which you blow out only to see them relight. Works every time . . . well until they (eventually) stop working. Everyone has a good

chuckle and then we all have to eat something pink and disgusting that's the sweetest thing known to mankind (and I don't mean that as a good thing).

So how do they actually work?

Well, you know when you light a candle? What you're actually lighting is the wick at the top. The wick of a trick candle has small amounts of magnesium in it – a highly flammable metal. So when you light the candle, you're also lighting the magnesium. When someone tries to blow out the flame, the magnesium inside the wick continues to burn and, a second later, relights the wick.

Why do my parents – and especially my grandparents – complain about school dinners?

My children could never understand why I would always make a face when they mentioned school dinners. They liked them

– and, hey, what wasn't to like! Pizza, pasta, salads: they all added up to the sort of menu that anyone would be happy to eat anywhere at any time.

It wasn't always like that.
Oh, no, no, no.

Your parents and grandparents had to endure absolute muck, I'm sorry but there are no other words to describe the rubbish that was put in front of us.

Here are some of the ghastly dishes we were obliged to eat:

- **Mince and carrots (flavourless mince in a watery gravy with almost-pureed carrots that your teacher made you eat).**

- Tapioca (aka frog spawn).

- **Spam (yeugh).**

- Spotted dick (with lumpy custard).

- **Toad-in-the-hole (all hole – no toad)**

- Macaroni cheese (with congealed cheese).

- **Rice pudding (with evil skin on top).**

Semolina (with the tiniest amount of jam).

- **Treacle pudding (heavy on the suet; light on the treacle).**

- Meat and two veg (fat, greens that had been boiled for four hours and boiled potatoes as hard as rocks).

Mere words can't do justice to it: I can still taste it. Well, actually I can't but you know what I mean.

And don't forget that, in those days, there was NO choice of food AND we HAD to 'clean our plates': i.e. we had to finish EVERYTHING that was dumped in front of us.

I still remember Mrs Pickering (who was otherwise a fine teacher) getting a jar of animal innards from her butcher, which she placed in front of her at lunchtime telling us that we would have to eat them if we didn't finish our meals.

True, she never actually made anyone eat those innards but then I can't remember ANYONE ever refusing to finish their food.

Why is a happy person said to be on 'cloud nine'?

'Look at him: he's so happy, he's on cloud nine!'

I don't know if you've ever heard this expression, but I'd be very surprised if you don't notice it the next time you hear it! But why cloud nine – why not cloud eight or cloud 979?

The answer is that cloud nine is based on terminology used by the US Weather Bureau. Clouds are divided into classes and each class is divided into nine types with level (or cloud) nine being the very highest. Such clouds can reach as high as 10,000 metres or even higher and appear as glorious white mountains in the sky. So if you were on cloud nine you'd be right at the top. And that's why it's used to describe a happy person.

What is the Exchequer – as in the Chancellor of the Exchequer?

In the days before calculators – and, dear reader, I am old enough to remember such a time – we used to do big sums in all sorts of different ways: from slide rules and abacuses to log tables (ask your grandparents what they were and stand by to watch them groan out loud), people did what they had to.

The office that looked after the country's money was no different. From the 12th century onwards, officials used a chequered cloth and counters to make their calculations with, and although this stopped in the 19th century, the place where they worked had become known as the Exchequer, from the squared cloth, and this name survived to form part of the Chancellor's title.

Which is the best British beach for building sandcastles?

According to a study done by students at Bournemouth University, Torre Abbey Sands in Torquay, Devon is the best beach in the country for sandcastles. It has extremely fine-grained sand with exceptional cohesive (binding) powers. Other sandcastle-friendly beaches are Bridlington, Great Yarmouth,

Bournemouth and Tenby.

For the best sandcastles you need eight parts sand to one part water.

But beware! Sandcastles can be really dangerous. They can even cause death – especially when people fall into the holes they've dug.

Why is a rich person described as well-heeled?

There are many possible answers to this question but the one I prefer is that it comes from the barbaric practice of cockfighting, which is now (thankfully) against the law. In the early days of this vile activity, the owners would sometimes add spurs to the feet of their birds, putting them at an advantage. Such birds were said to be 'well-heeled' and birds that didn't have spurs were said to be 'naked-heeled'.

Obviously, it could also be derived from the

fact that wealthy people would have decent heels on their shoes, but that doesn't make nearly as much sense. After all, if you wanted to use shoes as a metaphor for wealth, then why not say that someone was 'well-shod'?

Is/was there any connection between the American Dennis the Menace and the British Dennis the Menace?

Absolutely no connection, but one incredible coincidence. The American Dennis (Mitchell) – later the star of his own TV series – and the British Dennis, a star of The Beano comic were created just three days apart in March 1951. Their two creators – Hank Ketcham (in the US) and David Law (in the UK) – were unaware of each other's cartoons. When they found out, they agreed to carry on without reference to each other. To complete the coincidence, both Dennis the Menace characters wore striped jerseys.

Is it true that a composer once composed a piece that was just silence?

Yes, it is! Rather like an artist exhibiting a blank canvas as a work of art, an American avant-garde composer named John Cage composed 4′ 33″ which consisted of, er, four minutes and thirty-three seconds of total silence.

On 29 August 1952, this work was given its debut in Woodstock, New York. The instruction for the musician(s) was simple and concise: don't play a single note for the entire piece! The pianist David Tudor marked the beginning of the piece by closing the lid of the piano. He then opened it at the end of the first 'movement' and then repeated his actions for the second and third movements. The idea was for the audience to listen to the sounds of the ambient environment rather than the silence but, in any event, it was clearly an exploration of the question 'what is music?' – rather like Carl Andre's bricks raised the question What is art?

❋ As a tribute to John Cage here is a cartoon called 'Nothing in particular.'

Thank you!

In 2010, there was a Facebook campaign to get people to buy a recording of 4'33" in an attempt to deny The X Factor winner the number one Christmas single. It resulted in the 'record' getting to No. 21 in the charts, which isn't bad for silence!

Why do we give someone we don't like – or whom we wish to avoid – the cold shoulder?

You've probably had it happen to you. You'll go up to someone in the playground and they'll turn their back on you and ignore you. You'll be understandably upset and surprised. When you mention it to your parents, they'll say 'Do you know why they gave you the cold shoulder?'

I'd always thought it was one of those phrases that was self-explanatory: in other words, you were literally given a cold shoulder by someone who didn't want anything to do with you. Instead, I find that it has its roots in something quite specific. In olden times, when an unwanted visitor came you gave them cold shoulder of mutton instead of hot meat as a hint that they were not to call again.

So, Mitch, what's annoying you now?

In my last questions-and-answers book – the Blue Peter-award-winning *Do Igloos Have Loos* – I included the question: *You're a pretty reasonable chap, Mitch – is there anything that annoys you?* which I then proceeded to answer with a long list of gripes and peeves. You'd have thought that that would have been the end of things – that I would have absolutely nothing left to complain about – but that's to reckon without my legendary grumpiness. So here is another list of things that really annoy me.

- Being caught talking to myself. Happens more often than I'd like to admit.

- TV sports programmes using pop music as

a background to great goals or spectacular tries.

- People driving 4x4s when they're never going to go off-road.

- Artifically whitened teeth (very scary).

TV ads for ear wax softeners. Even worse
while we're eating.

- People who care what brand of mineral
water they're drinking. They wouldn't be
able to identify it in a blind tasting, the
idiots: it's all in the packaging.

- People who press 'Reply All' when they're
responding to jokey emails. You're not as
funny as you think you are, you know.

- Trumpets in the crowd at England football
matches.

- The design of our bodies. For example:
having arms too short to scratch the middle
of our backs.

- Tiny print on packets of food. What are
they trying to hide?

- Ice cream that is too hard to scoop out.

- The use of animal products – like the lining
of a cow's stomach – in foods like cheese
or Christmas pudding that could (and

should) be suitable for vegetarians.

- The words 'Warning: May contain traces of nuts' on products that obviously contain nuts (e.g. peanut butter).

- People with bad breath who insist on sharing it with us. Please feel free not to.

Cereal boxes and packets that are meant to be resealable but aren't.

- People confusing the words 'your' and 'you're'.

- Writers who use their initials instead of their first names. I've got a truly stupid first name and I don't.

- People nagging me to go on Fun Runs. Never was there a greater oxymoron than the expression 'fun run'.

- Footballers feigning injury during a match – i.e. cheating on their fellow professionals.

- British beaches polluted by raw sewage.

- Shops that have year-round sales. They're a con.

- People who call Christmas 'Crimbo'. Happens more than you think.

- Spam emails masquerading as personal ones: 'Hi Mitch, how are you?'

- The silly prices charged for sweets and drinks in multiplex cinemas.

- High street shops that put placards out in the middle of the street for us to trip over.

Train journeys that are more expensive than flights to the same destination.

- Mobile phone conversations held at full volume on public transport. We know you're on the train because we too are on the train. As for the person you're talking to, do they really need to know? I mean, you haven't just tunnelled out of Stalag Luft III in The Great Escape, have you?

- Spectators at golf tournaments who shout 'get in the hole!' at the ball – especially after a tee shot.

- People to whom you tell your name and who then say it back to you – wrongly. As though their guess is as good as yours.

- Vs in Scrabble. It's easier to place the Z, Q, X or J than the V, which is the only letter that doesn't appear in a two-letter word.

Questions I couldn't answer

In previous books in this series-within-a-series, I've given you a list of some of the questions I couldn't answer. Highlights (although the word 'lowlights' is equally valid) include:

- If a vegetarian eats vegetables, what does a humanitarian eat?

If corn oil is made from corn, what is baby oil made from?

- If you try to fail, and succeed, which have you done?

- Why do floorboards only creak at night?

- Why can't you buy a tube of toothpaste without an extra 10 per cent free?

- Why is it that when two planes almost hit each other it's called a 'near miss' when it's really a 'near hit'?

- Is clumsiness catching – or is it dropping?

- How can a product be described as 'new and improved'? If it's new, it can't be an improvement.

- If many hands make light work, how come too many cooks spoil the broth?

- If a mime artist is arrested, does he have the right to remain silent?

- Why do Mums say 'I'll teach you to behave badly!'

Now here are some more questions I simply couldn't answer . . .

- Why do noses run but feet smell?

- Once you've seen one shopping centre, have you seen a mall?

- Why is it that writers write but fingers don't fing?

- If teachers taught, why didn't preachers praught?

- How can a slim chance and a fat chance be the same?

- Are those who jump off a bridge in Paris inSeine?

- Why are flats called apartments when they're all joined together?

- If the plural of tooth is teeth, why isn't the plural of booth, beeth?

- If you have a bunch of odds and ends and get rid of all but one of them, what do you call it?

- Does a backward poet write inverse?

- Does reading while sunbathing makes you well red?

- Can a bicycle stand on its own if it's two tired?

- If a clock is hungry, does it go back four seconds?

- Is the man who fell into an upholstery machine fully recovered?

- Do bakers trade bread recipes on a knead-to-know basis?

• Is vaccination a jab well done?

And finally . . .

• Is a midget fortune-teller who escapes from prison a small medium at large?

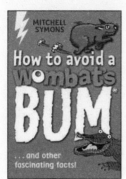

Mitchell Symons
HOW TO AVOID A WOMBAT'S BUM*
And other fascinating facts!

* Don't chase it! Wombats can run up to 25 miles per hour and stop dead in half a stride. They kill their predators this way – the predator runs into the wombat's bum-bone and smashes its face.

Amaze and intrigue your friends and family with more fantastic facts and figures:

- most dinosaurs were no bigger than chickens
- Everton was the first British football club to introduce a stripe down the side of players' shorts
- A snail has about 25,000 teeth
- No piece of paper can be folded in half more than seven times

Just opening this book will have you hooked for hours!

WORDS

'Stewardesses' is the longest word typed with only the left hand.

The only 15-letter word that does not repeat a letter is 'uncopyrightable'.

Shakespeare invented more than 1,700 words, including 'assassination' and 'bump'.

Hull City is the only British football team that hasn't got any letters you can fill in with a pen.

The ball on top of a flagpole is called the 'truck'.

Zenith, tariff, sherbet, algebra, carafe, coffee, syrup, cotton, mattress and alcohol are all words derived from Arabic.

'Knightsbridge' is the place name with the most consonants in a row.

Food that's spat out is called 'chanking'.

IOU doesn't stand for 'I owe you'. It stands for 'I owe unto'.

1,000 words make up 90 per cent of all writing.

A 'clue' originally meant a ball of thread. This is why you 'unravel the clues' of a mystery.

No word in the English language rhymes with orange, silver, month, pint or diamond.

Queue is the only word in the English language to be pronounced the same way even if the last four letters are removed.

The name 'jeep' came from the abbreviation 'GP', used in the army for general-purpose vehicle.

The letters 'ough' can be pronounced seven different ways in the following sentence: 'A rough, dough-faced, thoughtful ploughman walked through the streets of Scarborough, coughing.'

***Alice in Wonderland* author, Lewis Carroll, invented the word 'chortle' – a combination of 'chuckle' and 'snort'.**

'Taramasalata' (a type of Greek pâté) and 'Galatasaray' (name of a Turkish football club) each have an 'a' for every other letter.

ANIMALS

Most dinosaurs were no bigger than chickens.

A mouse has more bones than a human: mouse 225, human 206.

A newborn panda is smaller than a mouse.

The armadillo is the only animal – apart from man – that can catch leprosy.

A beaver can chop down more than 200 trees in a year.

Besides humans, the only animal that can suffer sunburn is the pig.

A skunk will not bite and throw its scent at the same time.

A rabbit takes about 18 naps a day.

Giant pandas can eat 38 kilograms of bamboo a day.

A dog can suffer from tonsillitis, but not appendicitis. It doesn't have an appendix.

A monkey was once tried and convicted for smoking a cigarette in Indiana.

At full speed, a cheetah takes eight-metre strides.

Koalas have no natural predators.

A rodent's teeth never stop growing.

A donkey will sink in quicksand but a mule won't.

Tigers have striped skin, not just striped fur.

Male monkeys go bald in much the same way that men do.

Polar bears can smell a human being from 20 miles away.

Polar bears cover their black noses with their paws for better camouflage.

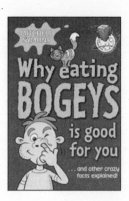

Mitchell Symons
WHY EATING BOGEYS IS GOOD FOR YOU

And other crazy facts explained!

Ever wondered . . .

- Why we have tonsils?
- Is there any cream in cream crackers?
- What's the best way to cure hiccups?
- And if kangaroos keep their babies in their pouches, what happens to all the poo?

Mitchell Symons answers all these wacky questions and plenty more in a wonderfully addictive book that will have you hooked for hours!

(And eating bogeys is good for you . . . but only your own!)

Selected for the Booktrust Booked Up! Initiative in 2008.

Why is the sea blue?

Do you want the difficult or the (relatively) simple explanation?

Yup, I thought so. Here goes then.

If you take a bucket of seawater, it is, of course, colourless. So how come it looks blue when there's lots of it? Well, obviously, there's the matter of the blue sky being reflected in the sea, but it's got much more to do with the sun's rays. The water absorbs all the sun's rays beating down on it. However, the redder colours in the spectrum get absorbed better than the bluer colours, and so you tend to get left with a combination of those blue colours (blue, indigo and violet), which changes according to the position of you and of the sun, and also according to the sun's intensity.

What's the best thing to do in a plummeting lift?

Pray. According to Dr Adrian Newman, a physicist, 'Assuming all the lift cables have gone, and assuming that the lift is falling at a speed of, say, 60 feet per second – or 40 miles per hour – there's nothing you can do to soften the impact. More to the point, at that sort of speed over that sort of distance, you are not going to get the time to think, let alone act. You're going to end up like a pancake.'

Is that it? What about jumping?

'Why?'

To minimize impact.

'Even if you had time to think, this would not be a good idea. You're travelling down at 40 miles per hour; how fast are you going to jump up – always assuming that you can time your jump just right? Four miles per hour? Five miles per hour? At best, you are still

travelling down at 40 minus 5 – at 35 miles per hour. You are still going to get splattered. Put it another way. Let's say you have a terminal velocity of 30 metres per second. Even if you were an Olympic athlete, you are only going to be able to leap up at a speed of 3 metres per second. So you are reducing your terminal velocity to 27 metres per second. It's like jumping from the 20th floor instead of the 22nd.'

Is there anything I can do? What about bracing myself or clinging to the sides?

'That's fine at slow speeds like five or ten miles per hour, and bending your knees will stop them being shoved up into your body, but in a plummeting lift that's useless. The best thing is to make sure that you only travel in lifts with very fat people so that if it does crash, there's a chance that they will cushion your fall!'

Mitchell Symons
HOW MUCH POO DOES AN ELEPHANT DO?*

... and further fascinating facts!

* An elephant produces an eye-wateringly pongy 20 kilograms of dung a day!

Let Mitchell Symons be your guide into the weird and wonderful world of trivia.

- Camels are born without humps
- Walt Disney, creator of Mickey Mouse, was scared of mice
- Only 30% of humans can flare their nostrils
- A group of twelve or more cows is called a flink

Notes sent by parents to school

Please excuse Joey on Friday; he had loose vowels.

Dear school: Please exkuse John for being absent on January 28, 29, 30, 31, 32 and 33.

Lillie was absent from school yesterday as she had a gang over.

Please excuse Johnnie for being. It was his father's fault.

I kept Billie home to do Christmas shopping because I didn't know what size she wears.

Please excuse Sara for being absent. She was sick and I had her shot.

Not what they seem

Catgut isn't made from cats, it's made from sheep.

Venetian blinds were invented in Japan, not Venice.

Camel-hair brushes are made from squirrel hair.

Soda water doesn't contain soda.

Turkish baths originated in ancient Rome, not in Turkey.

There wasn't a single pony in the Pony Express, only horses.

An ant lion is neither an ant nor a lion. (It is the larval form of the lacewing fly.)

Leaves don't change colour in autumn. They look green because they contain chlorophyll. When the leaf dies, the chlorophyll disappears and the other colours, which were there all along, emerge.

Animals

The South American giant anteater eats more than 30,000 ants a day.

Camel milk does not curdle.

A grasshopper needs a minimum air temperature of 16°C before it's able to hop.

Polar-bear liver contains so much vitamin A that it could be fatal to a human if eaten.

The greater dwarf lemur in Madagascar always gives birth to triplets.

Somalia has more goats than people.

Giraffes have no vocal cords.

An anaconda can swallow a pig.

Nearly all polar bears are left-handed.

The only country with a national dog is the Netherlands (the Keeshond).

There are no furry animals native to Antarctica.

A dzo is the offspring of a yak and a cow.

A geep is the offspring of a sheep and a goat.

Pigs can become addicted to alcohol.

Sir Anthony Hopkins (black-footed penguin) and Rolf Harris (koala) both 'adopted' animals at London Zoo.

The average porcupine has more than 30,000 quills. Porcupines are excellent swimmers. Their quills are hollow and act like floating aids.

Skunk litters are born in April.

Mitchell Symons
WHY DO FARTS SMELL LIKE ROTTEN EGGS?

. . . and more crazy facts explained!

Ever wondered . . .

- Why we burp?
- What a wotsit is?
- Whether lemmings really jump off cliffs?
- Why vomit always contains carrots?
- And why *do* farts smell like rotten eggs?

No subject is too strange and no trivia too tough for Mitchell Symons, who has the answers to these crazy questions, and many more.

Why is it considered bad luck to kill a ladybird?

Apart from the fact that they are beautiful creatures and therefore deserve to be protected, they pose no direct danger to humans whatsoever. After all, when was the last time YOU were stung by a ladybird. However, the reason why it's considered unlucky to kill one is because the ladybird is said to represent the Virgin Mary, and you wouldn't want to mess with Jesus' mum!

Given that money can do great good, why is it described as 'the root of all evil'?

Of course money isn't, *per se*, the root of all evil, in fact, that so-called quotation is wrong. The Bible doesn't say that 'money is the root of all evil', it says 'For the love of money is the root of all evil.' In other words, money itself is fine – but don't worship it!

Why do ostriches stick their heads in the sand?

People who don't want to face up to some unpleasant fact are often accused of sticking their heads in the sand like an ostrich. In fact, the (simple) reason why ostriches stick their heads in the sand is because they're looking for water – not trying to avoid something.

What are the origins of Rudolph, the red-nosed reindeer?

Rudolph was created as recently as 1939 for a Christmas promotion for the Montgomery Ward department store in Chicago. The words were written as a poem by Robert May, an advertising copywriter, but music wasn't added until 1947 – by which time May had persuaded the store to let him have the rights to the character. In 1949 Gene Autry recorded the song and had a massive hit with it.

Do Scotsmen wear anything under their kilts?

According to a Scottish friend I asked – a regular kilt-wearer: 'No, not if they're real Scotsmen.'

But what if the wind blows your kilt over your head . . . ?

'We wear special shirts that have long tails. On an especially windy day, we might tie up those tails to protect our modesty. But don't tell anyone that, OK?'

Your secret is safe with me . . . and my readers!

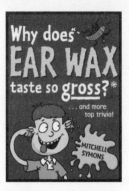

Mitchell Symons

WHY DOES EAR WAX TASTE SO GROSS?*

... and more top trivia!

*stinky ear wax has been hanging around in the ear canal for nearly a month before it is 'pickable'!

Did you know . . .

- **Humans share a third of their DNA with lettuce**

- **Cockroaches fart every fifteen minutes**

- **Giraffes never kneel**

- **The average person spends six months of their life on the loo**

Amaze your mates and fascinate your family with this book packed with jaw-dropping, eyebrow-raising facts!

Creepy crawlies

Bees can recognize human faces.

There are 350,000 known species of beetle – with millions more waiting for names.

The giant cricket eats human hair.

Butterfly hunters in the 19th century used to line their top hats with cork so they had somewhere to pin the butterflies they'd caught.

Female scorpions sometimes eat their own offspring.

The average spider will spin more than four miles of silk in a lifetime.

One in four creatures on earth is a beetle.

In Britain in the past 10 years, farmland butterflies have declined by 30 per cent.

Insect flatulence – that's farting to you and me – accounts for up to a fifth of all the methane emissions on the planet.

Fire ants have adapted to cope with flooding. When water levels in their nests rise, they form a huge ball with the workers on the outside and the queen inside. This ball then floats to higher ground, where they wait for the water to go down.

The male scorpion fly gets other males to bring him food by imitating the sound of a female fly.

Some moths survive by drinking the salty tears of cattle.

Fish

There are about 21,000 varieties of fish on earth.

The Dover sole uses the sound of the wind above the waves to know where it is and where it's going.

The oldest known goldfish was Goldie, who lived for 45 years after being won at a fairground in 1960.

Mudfish can survive in mud for a year until

the rain comes.

If a goldfish is exposed to a loud noise, it can take a month for its hearing to get back to normal.

Three-quarters of a fish is eaten – the rest is used to make things such as glue, soap, margarine and fertilizer.

An electric eel can produce an average of 400 volts. Its electric organs make up four-fifths of its body.

The flounder swims sideways.

Swordfish can heat up their eyeballs to help them see when they go hunting.

Even though cuttlefish are colour-blind, they can change colour to camouflage themselves.

The bream, a freshwater fish, hatches its eggs in its mouth.

When common eels lay their eggs, they die.

Mitchell Symons

WHY YOU NEED A PASSPORT WHEN YOU'RE GOING TO PUKE*

. . . and more crazy-but-true facts!

*Puke is the name of a town in Albania. Would YOU like to holiday there . . . ?

Did you know . . .

- **Square watermelons are sold in Japan**

- **There is a River Piddle in Dorset**

- **American use enough toilet paper daily to wrap around the world nine times**

Mitchell Symons goes global – join him on his fun fact-finding world tour!

Fascinating facts!

There's a river in Nicaragua called the Pis Pis River.

There was once an internet rumour that Belgium doesn't exist. That's right, that Belgium – as in the country – doesn't exist. I'll believe it if you do!

The first astronauts to go to the Moon trained in Iceland because the terrain there was reckoned to be similar to the Moon's surface.

Mozambique has all five vowels in it.

If you buy a map of South America in Peru, it'll differ from one sold in Ecuador. This is because there's a big row between the two countries as to who owns the area around the Amazon headwater.

There is no known case of a vegetarian dying from a snake bite in America.

Liechtenstein used to have the world's smallest army. There was one soldier. He served his country faithfully until his death at the age of 95. Then Liechtenstein went from having the world's smallest army to no army at all.

Waikikamukau – pronounced 'Why kick a moo cow?' – is the expression New Zealanders use for a particularly remote rural town. Sadly, there's no actual place with that name!

Girls and women aren't allowed to walk on Mount Athos in Macedonia. In fact, even female animals are not allowed there.

There are people who claim that it's illegal to dress up as Batman in Australia. This is because of an obscure law which prohibits the wearing of dark clothes all over the body for fear that someone will look like a cat burglar. Given that the Batman costume is pretty much all black, some people insist that it is covered by this law and that therefore it must be illegal to dress up as Batman.

In Tibet, some women have special metal instruments they use for picking their noses.

Tobago was Daniel Defoe's inspiration for the island which Robinson Crusoe found himself washed up on.

In the 19th century a French mime artist accidentally got stuck in his imaginary glass box and starved to death. Think about it . . .

There was once a Togolese man with 17 wives and 60 children.

Genuine dishes from around the world

Stir-fried Dog (China)

Rabbit Excrement (Red Indians of Lake Superior used this as a flavouring in red wine)

Minced Giant Bullfrog Savoury Sandwich Spread (US)

Deep-fried Horsemeat (Switzerland)

Mixed Organ (spleen, pancreas, aorta, etc.)

Beef Stew (Austria)

Caterpillar Lava Of The Large Pandora Moth (Pai-utes Indians of Oregon)

Roast Wallaby (Australia)

Calf's Head with Brain Fritters (19th-century US)

Steamed Cat and Chicken (China)

Burgoo (squirrel, rabbit, pigeon, wild duck and/or chicken, vegetables stew) (U.S. Appalachian)

Bandicoote Stewed In Milk (Australia - early 20th century)

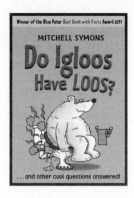

Mitchell Symons

DO IGLOOS HAVE LOOS?

Ever wondered . . .

- Why are slugs so slimy?

- **Why does your skin go wrinkly in the bath?**

- How clever is your right foot?

- **What is the best thing to do if you fall into quicksand?**

- And do igloos have loos?

Mitchell Symons knows the answers . . . and now you will too!

UGGY POTTER AND THE CAVEMAN'S STONE

What was the first ever children's book?

First of all, let's exclude school books –
on the basis that there would have been
handwritten books for princes to use for
studying.

The first ever children's book – printed in English – was a 1563 book of rhymes entitled *A Book in Englyshh Metre of the Great Merchant Man Called Dives Pragmaticus*. Consisting of just eight pages, it contained rhymes about Mr Dives Pragmaticus's business, and so not only was it the first children's book, it was also probably the first example of product placement in the media!

Are hot drinks more cooling than cold drinks when the weather's hot?

You'd think that a cold drink would cool you down, wouldn't you? Certainly, when it's hot, I find myself craving something cold in a glass full of ice.

However, this isn't necessarily a good idea. It might make you *think* you're cooling down but – apart from the rehydration your body obviously craves – it's doubtful whether it's actually doing anything to make you cooler.

And, indeed, there's the potential problem that if you drink a very cold drink too fast on a hot day, you might get stomach cramps.

In fact, when it comes to cooling down, it's not just a question of counteracting the outside air temperature (which is what a cold drink seems to do). What you're looking for is something to make you sweat and, if you like, match up your temperature inside and out.

A hot drink makes you sweat, which in turn takes heat away from your body and cools you down.

If you want further proof of this, then look at India, a country that experiences extremely high temperatures. There they drink cups of hot tea to keep cool. We'd be wise to follow their lead on this.

Mitchell Symons

ON YOUR FARTS, GET SET, GO!

Mitchell Symons has stats and stories to entertain and amaze you!

- Did the Ancient Olympians really compete in the buff?

- **Which striker's shorts fell down when he was taking a penalty?**

- Which sport consists of running while juggling?

- **Which football team's fanzine is called *Linesman, You're Rubbish*?**

Mitchell Symons knows the answers . . . and now you will too!

Lasts

The last Olympics in which the gold medals were made entirely of gold were in 1912.

The last time a First Division or Premiership club had two players scoring more than 30 goals in a season was Sunderland in 1935–36, when Raich Carter and Bob Gurney each scored 31 goals.

Eight-ball overs were last used at Test level in 1978–79 in Australia and New Zealand.

In 1932–33 Dennis Smith of New Zealand dismissed Eddie Paynter of England with his very first ball in Test cricket. Unfortunately for Dennis, it wasn't just his first wicket in Test cricket but also his last as he never took another!

Every year the football teams of England, Scotland, Wales and Northern Ireland competed for the British Championship. The last one was in the 1983–84 season, and Northern Ireland won – for only the third time in their history – and so kept the trophy.

Oops!

When Celestine Babayaro made his debut for Chelsea in a pre-season match, he was thrilled to score – so thrilled that he broke his leg while celebrating, putting him out of action for much of the season.

English referee Graham Poll mistakenly handed out *three* yellow cards to Croatia's Josip Šimuni in a 2006 football World Cup match against Australia.

The great South African golfer Gary Player was once accused of being lucky. 'That's funny,' he replied. 'The harder I practise, the luckier I get.' Fabulous response, but obviously he could have used a bit more practice in a 1955 tournament in Huddersfield, England. At the final hole he was in the lead and needed just a par four to win. His second shot landed near the green, a few inches from a stone wall. Because there

was no room for a backswing and Player didn't want to waste a stroke knocking the ball clear of the wall, he decided to make the ball ricochet off the wall. It didn't work out exactly the way he planned. The ball bounced back and hit him in the face. Player was not only hurt but was also penalized two strokes for 'impeding the flight of the ball' – and duly lost the tournament. All together now . . . oops!

Mitchell Symons

DON'T WIPE YOUR BUM WITH A HEDGEHOG

Top tips from the marvellous mind of Mitchell Symons.

- Why buy shampoo when real poo is free?

- **Never put both your feet in your mouth as you won't have a leg to stand on.**

- You can't trust a dog to watch your food.

- **And if getting even doesn't work, just get odd!**

Mitchell Symons knows the answers . . . and now you will too!

NOXIOUS NOISY AND STINKY SMELLS,

FRIGHTFUL FACTS AND GORY STORIES,

GO MAD FOR MINIBEASTS,
IT'S A JUNGLE OUT THERE

heaven in

National
Gallery

heaven in

art

National
Gallery

Sandro Botticelli: detail of *Mystic Nativity*

Published in Great Britain 1998
by Weidenfeld & Nicolson
The Orion Publishing Group
Orion House
5 Upper St Martin's Lane
London WC2H 9EA

A CIP catalogue for this book is available from the British Library
ISBN: 0 297 82474 0

Series Editor: Ljiljana Ortolja-Baird
Designer: Bet Ayer
Typeset in: DeVinne

Title page: Garofalo, detail of *Saint Augustine and the Holy Family
and Saint Catherine of Alexandria ('The Vision of Saint Augustine')*

Fra Filippo Lippi: detail of *Seven Saints*

Guido Reni: detail of *The Coronation of the Virgin*

INTRODUCTION

'As painting, so poetry'. Like all siblings, the Sister Arts are rivals and allies. In the mirrors they hold up to nature we see ourselves reflected from varying angles and by different lights.

The National Gallery in London is home to many of the world's finest European paintings. For hundreds of years, the main task of such paintings was to assist Christian devotion: to make the invisible tenets of faith visible to plain sight. Above all, the artists strove to surpass the evocative power of the words spoken and sung by prophets, mystics and poets, by depicting, in precious materials and with exquisite craft, the resplendence of Heaven, the ineffable tenderness of divine love and the fortitude of saints.

By exploring each painting in detail, often finding aspects that we never 'knew' were there, *Heaven in Art* is an intimate voyage of discovery. We do not need to be devout, or even believers, to delight in the vivid and beautiful texts and images so aptly paired in this book.

Erika Langmuir
Head of Education, National Gallery, 1988–1995

7

messengers
of grace

9

SANDRO BOTTICELLI (about 1445–1510) Italian
'Mystic Nativity'
1500

Angels we have heard on high
Sweetly singing o'er the plains,
And the mountains in reply
Echoing their joyous strains:
Gloria in excelsis Deo,
Gloria in excelsis Deo.

Shepherds why this jubilee?
Why your joyous strains prolong?
What the gladsome tidings be
Which inspire your heav'nly song?
Gloria in excelsis Deo,
Gloria in excelsis Deo.

Come to Bethlehem and see
Him whose birth the angels sing.
Come adore on bended knee
Christ the Lord, the new-born King.
Gloria in excelsis Deo,
Gloria in excelsis Deo.

Angels We Have Heard on High,
ANONYMOUS, Traditional English Carol, 1855

11

13

14

15

DUCCIO (active 1278; died 1318/19) Italian
The Annunciation
1311

The angel and the girl are met.
Earth was the only meeting place.
For the embodied never yet
Travelled beyond the shore of space.
The eternal spirits in freedom go.

See, they have come together, see,
While the destroying minutes flow,
Each reflects the other's face
Till heaven in hers and earth in his
Shine steady there. He's come to her
From far beyond the farthest star,
Feathered through time. Immediacy
Of strangest strangeness is the bliss
That from their limbs all movement takes.
Yet the increasing rapture brings
So great a wonder that it makes
Each feather tremble on his wings.

Outside the window footsteps fall
Into the ordinary day
And with the sun along the wall
Pursue their unreturning way.
Sound's perpetual roundabout

17

Rolls its numbered octaves out
And hoarsely grinds its battered tune.

But through the endless afternoon
These neither speak nor movement make,
But stare into their deepening trance
As if their gaze would never break.

The Annunciation,
EDWIN MUIR, 1956

19

ASSOCIATE OF LEONARDO DA VINCI
(Leonardo da Vinci, 1452–1519, Italian)
An Angel in Red with a Lute
probably about 1490–99

In Heaven a spirit doth dwell
   'Whose heart-strings are a lute;'
None sing so wildly well
As the angel Israfel,
And the giddy stars (so legends tell)
Ceasing their hymns, attend the spell
   Of his voice, all mute.

Tottering above
   In her highest noon,
   The enamoured moon
Blushes with love,
   While, to listen, the red levin
   (With the rapid Pleiads, even,
   Which were seven)
   Pauses in Heaven.

And they say (the starry choir
   And the other listening things)
 That Israfeli's fire
Is owing to that lyre
   By which he sits and sings—
The trembling living wire
   Of those unusual strings.

But the skies that angel trod,
  Where deep thoughts are a duty,
Where Love's a grown-up God,
  Where the Houri glances are
Imbued with all the beauty
  Which we worship in a star.

Therefore, thou art not wrong,
  Israfeli, who despisest
An unimpassioned song;
  To thee the laurels belong,
  Best bard, because the wisest!
Merrily live, and long!

from *Israfel*,
EDGAR ALLAN POE, 1831

23

PHILIPPE DE CHAMPAIGNE
(1602–1674) French
The Vision of Saint Joseph
about 1638

As Joseph was a-walking
  He heard an Angel sing:
'This night there shall be born
  Our gracious Heav'nly King;
He neither shall be born
  In housen nor in hall,
Nor in the place of Paradise,
  But in an ox's stall.'

'He neither shall be christen'd
  In white wine nor in red;
But with the fair spring water,
  With which we were christenèd.'
As Joseph was a-walking,
  Thus did the Angel sing;
And Mary's Child at midnight
  Was born to be our King.

from *As Joseph Was A-walking*,
ANONYMOUS, Traditional French Carol

25

After Adam Elsheimer

(Adam Elsheimer, 1578–1610, German)

Tobias and the Archangel Raphael returning with the Fish
mid-17th century

At last I made bold to ask him to tell us who he was.

'An angel,' he said, quite simply, and set another bird free
and clapped his hands and made it fly away.

A kind of awe fell upon us when we heard him say that,
and we were afraid again; but he said we need not be
troubled, there was no occasion for us to be afraid of an
angel, and he liked us, anyway. He went on chatting as
simply and unaffectedly as ever…Then Seppi asked him
what his own name was, and he said, tranquilly, 'Satan'…

It caught us suddenly, that name did, and our work dropped out of our hands and broke to pieces…Satan laughed, and asked what was the matter. I said, 'Nothing, only it seemed a strange name for an angel.' He asked why.

'Because it's – it's – well, it's his name, you know.'

'Yes – he is my uncle.'

He said it placidly, but it took our breath for a moment and made our hearts beat…'Don't you remember? – he was an angel himself, once.'

'Yes – it's true,' said Seppi; 'I didn't think of that.'

'Before the Fall he was blameless.'

'Yes,' said Nikolaus, 'he was without sin.'

'It is a good family – ours,' said Satan; 'there is not a better. He is the only member of it that has ever sinned.'

from *The Mysterious Stranger*,
MARK TWAIN, published 1916

The Wilton Diptych

Richard II presented to the Virgin and Child by his Patron
Saint John the Baptist and Saints Edward and Edmund
about 1395–99

Let them praise Thy Name, let them praise Thee, the
supercelestial people, Thine angels, who have no need to
gaze up at this firmament, or by reading to know of Thy
word. For they always behold Thy face, and there read without any syllables in time, what willeth Thy eternal will; they
read, they choose, they love. They are ever reading; and that
never passes away which they read; for by choosing, and by
loving, they read the very unchangeableness of Thy counsel.
Their book is never closed, nor their scroll folded up; seeing
Thou Thyself art this to them, and art eternally; because
Thou hast ordained them above this firmament, which Thou
hast firmly settled over the infirmity of the lower people,
where they may gaze up and learn Thy mercy, announcing in
time Thee Who madest times. For Thy mercy, O Lord, is in
the heavens, and Thy truth reacheth unto the clouds. The
clouds pass away, but the heaven abideth.

from *Confessions*,
SAINT AUGUSTINE, about 400

32

33

34

35

FRANCESCO BOTTICINI
(about 1446–1497) Italian
The Assumption of the Virgin
probably about 1475–76

And at that centre, with their wings expanded,
  More than a thousand jubilant Angels saw I,
  Each differing in effulgence and in kind.
I saw there at their sports and at their songs
  A beauty smiling, which the gladness was
  Within the eyes of all the other saints;
And if I had in speaking as much wealth
  As in imagining, I should not dare
  To attempt the smallest part of its delight.

from 'Paradiso', *Divina Commedia*
DANTE, 1318–21

LORENZO COSTA (about 1459/60–1535) Italian
The Adoration of the Shepherds with Angels
about 1499

Run, shepherds, run where Bethlem blest appears,
We bring the best of news, be not dismayed,
A Saviour there is born more old than years,
Amidst heaven's rolling heights this earth who stayed:
In a poor cottage inned, a virgin maid
A weakling did him bear, who all upbears;
There is he, poor swaddled, in a manger laid,
To whom too narrow swaddlings are our spheres:
Run, shepherds , run, and solemnize his birth,
This is that night – no, day, grown great with bliss,
In which the power of Satan broken is;
In heaven be glory, peace unto earth!
   Thus singing, through the air the angels swam,
   And cope of stars re-echoed the same.

The Angels for the Nativity of our Lord,
WILLIAM DRUMMOND, early 17th century

40

41

43

the light of
the world

45

GEERTGEN TOT SINT JANS
(about 1455–65; died about 1485–95) Dutch
The Nativity, at Night
late 15th century

Mary was watching tenderly
  Her little son;
Softly the mother sang to sleep
  Her darling one.
Sleep, lovely Child, be now at rest,
  Thou Son of Light;
Sleep, pretty fledgling, in Thy nest
  All thro' the night.

Mary has spread your manger bed,
  Sleep, little Dove,
God's creatures all draw near to praise,
  Crown of my love.
Sleep little Pearl, Creator, Lord,
  Our homage take;
Bees bring you honey from their hoard,
  When you wake.

Mary Was Watching,
ANONYMOUS, Traditional Czech Carol

46

47

49

JAN GOSSAERT (active 1503; died 1532) Flemish
The Adoration of the Kings
1500–15

Now as at all times I can see in the mind's eye,
In their stiff, painted clothes, the pale unsatisfied ones
Appear and disappear in the blue depth of the sky
With all their ancient faces like rain-beaten stones,
And all their helms of silver hovering side by side,
And all their eyes still fixed, hoping to find once more,
Being by Calvary's turbulence unsatisfied,
The uncontrollable mystery on the bestial floor.

The Magi,
WILLIAM BUTLER YEATS, 1914

FEDERICO BAROCCI (1535–1612) Italian
The Madonna and Child with Saint Joseph and the Infant
Baptist (La Madonna del Gatto)
probably about 1575

See what a charming smile I bring,
Which no one can resist;
For I have a wondrous thing—
The Fact that I exist.

And I have found another, which
I now proceed to tell.
The world is so sublimely rich
That you exist as well.

Fact One is lovely, so is Two,
But O the best is Three:
The fact that I can smile at you,
And you can smile at me.

The Plain Facts, By a PLAIN but AMIABLE Cat,
RUTH PITTER, 20th century

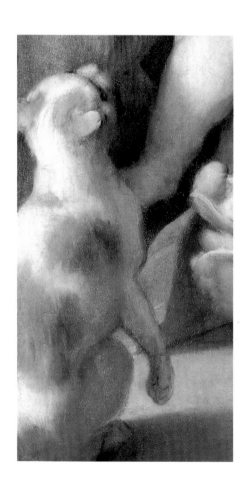

56

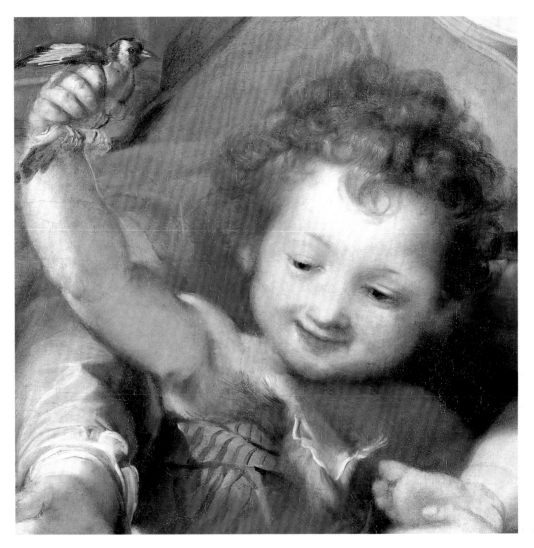

57

58

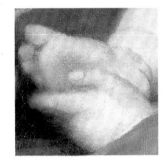

59

GUIDO RENI (1575–1642) Italian
Christ embracing Saint John the Baptist
about 1640

You, through whose face
all lovely faces look,
and are resolved for ever
in your soul's true mirror:
you, in whose unspoken words
the irrevocable voices speak again,
making in this less divided moment
the remembered music that the heart accords.

O you who are myself and yet another,
who are the world, and the unknown
through which the town, the river,
the familiar gardens and the fountain shines;
here is my hand, and with it let all hands
be given, and be held, in yours and mine.

Meeting with a Stranger,
JAMES KIRKUP, 1947

61

63

HANS BALDUNG GRIEN (1484/5–1545) German
The Trinity and Mystic Pietà
1512

Yes, love (he thought again with perfect distinctness), but
not that love that loves for something, to gain something, or
because of something, but that love that I felt for the first
time, when dying, I saw my enemy and yet loved him. I knew
that feeling of love which is the very essence of the soul, for
which no object is needed. And I know that blissful feeling
now too. To love one's neighbours; to love one's enemies. To
love everything – to love God in all His manifestations. Some
one dear to one can be loved with human love; but an enemy
can only be loved with divine love. And that was why I felt
such joy when I felt that I loved that man. What happened
to him? Is he still alive?…Loving with human love, one may
pass from love to hatred; but divine love cannot change.
Nothing, not even death, nothing can shatter it. It is the
very nature of the soul…

Love is life. All, all that I understand, I understand only
because I love. All is, all exists only because I love. All is
bound up in love alone. Love is God, and dying means for me
a particle of love, to go back to the universal and eternal
source of love.

from *War and Peace*,
LEO TOLSTOY, 1863–69

65

FRA ANGELICO (about 1395–1455) Italian
Christ Glorified in the Court of Heaven
probably 1428–30

The Lord is king, with majesty enrobed;
the Lord has robed himself with might,
he has girded himself with power.

The world you made firm, not to be moved;
your throne has stood firm from of old.
From all eternity, O Lord, you are.

The waters have lifted up, O Lord,
the waters have lifted up their voice,
the waters have lifted up their thunder.

Greater than the roar of mighty waters,
more glorious than the surgings of the sea,
the Lord is glorious on high.

Truly your decrees are to be trusted.
Holiness is fitting to your house,
O Lord, until the end of time.

Psalm 93

71

queen of
heaven

I sing of a maiden
   That is matchless.
King of all kings
   For her son she chose.

He came all so still
   Where his mother was,
As dew in April
   That falleth on the grass.

He came all so still
   To his mother's bower,
As dew in April
   That falleth on the flower.

He came all so still–
   There his mother lay,
As dew in April
   That falleth on the spray.

Mother and maiden
   Was never none but she;
Well may such a lady
   God's mother be.

Mother and Maiden,
ANONYMOUS, early 16th century

77

POVSSIN·FACIEBAT·
ANNO·SALVTIS·MDCLVII·
ALEX·SEPT·PONT·MAX·REGNANTE·
·ROMA·

NICOLAS POUSSIN (1594–1665) French
The Annunciation
1657

Waking alone in a multitude of loves when morning's light
Surprised in the opening of her nightlong eyes
His golden yesterday asleep upon the iris
And this day's sun leapt up the sky out of her thighs
Was miraculous virginity old as loaves and fishes,
Though the moment of a miracle is unending lightning
And the shipyards of Galilee's footprints hide a navy
    of doves.

from *On the Marriage of a Virgin*,
DYLAN THOMAS, 1946

85

MARGARITO OF AREZZO
(active 1262?) Italian
The Virgin and Child Enthroned, with
Scenes of the Nativity and the Lives of the Saints
1260s

Our Lady, too small for her canopy,
Sits near the altar. There's no comeliness
At all or charm in that expressionless
Face with its heavy eyelids. As before,
This face, for centuries a memory,
Non est species, neque decor,
Expressionless, expresses God: it goes
Past castled Sion. She knows what God knows,
Not Calvary's Cross nor crib at Bethlehem
Now, and the world shall come to Walsingham.

from *Our Lady of Walsingham,*
ROBERT LOWELL, 1946

90

ATTRIBUTED TO JAN PROVOOST
(living 1491; died 1529) Flemish
The Virgin and Child in a Landscape
early 16th century

A baby is born us bliss to bring;
A maiden I heard lullay sing:
'Dear son, now leave thy weeping,
Thy father is the king of bliss.'

'Nay, dear mother, for you weep I not,
But for thinges that shall be wrought
Or that I have mankind i-bought:
Was there never pain like it iwis.'

'Peace, dear son, say thou me not so.
Thou art my child, I have no mo.
Alas! that I should see this woe:
It were to me great heaviness.'

'My handes, mother, that ye now see,
They shall be nailéd on a tree;
My feet, also, fastened shall be:
Full many shall weep that it shall see.'

'Alas! dear son, sorrow is now my hap;
To see the child that sucks my pap
So ruthfully taken out of my lap:
It were to me great heaviness.'

'Also, mother, there shall a spear
My tendere heart all to-tear;
The blood shall cover my body there:
Great ruthe it shall be to see.'

'Ah! dear son, that is a heavy case.
When Gabriel kneeled before my face
And said, "Hail! Lady, full of grace,"
He never told me nothing of this.'

'Dear mother, peace, now I you pray,
And take no sorrow for that I say,
But sing this song, "By, by, lullay,"
To drive away all heaviness.'

A Baby is Born,
ANONYMOUS, 15th century

94

JUAN DE VALDES LEAL (1622–1690) Spanish
The Immaculate Conception of the Virgin, with Two Donors
probably 1661

WILD air, world-mothering air,
Nestling me everywhere,
That each eyelash or hair
Girdles; goes home betwixt
The fleeciest, frailest-flixed
Snowflake; that's fairly mixed
With, riddles, and is rife
In every least thing's life;
This needful, never spent,
And nursing element;
My more than meat and drink,
My meal at every wink;
This air, which, by life's law,
My lung must draw and draw
Now but to breathe its praise,
Minds me in many ways
Of her who not only
Gave God's infinity
Dwindled to infancy
Welcome in womb and breast,
Birth, milk, and all the rest
But mothers each new grace
That does now reach our race—

Mary Immaculate,
Merely a woman, yet
Whose presence, power is
Great as no goddess's
Was deemèd, dreamèd; who
This one work has to do—
Let all God's glory through,
God's glory which would go
Through her and from her flow
Off, and no way but so.

    I say that we are wound
With mercy round and round
As if with air: the same
Is Mary, more by name.
She, wild web, wondrous robe,
Mantles the guilty globe,
Since God has let dispense
Her prayers his providence:
Nay, more than almoner,
The sweet alms' self is her
And men are meant to share
Her life as life does air.

from The Blessed Virgin
compared to the Air we Breathe,
GERARD MANLEY HOPKINS, 1883

99

Guido Reni (1575–1642)
Italian
The Coronation of the Virgin
about 1607

Lady, flower of alle thing,
   Rosa sine spina,
Thou bore Jesu, heavenes king,
   Gratia divina.
Of alle thou bear'st the prize,
Lady, queen of Paradise
   Electa.

from *In Praise of Mary*,
Anonymous, 13th century

saints

FRA FILIPPO LIPPI
(born about 1406; died 1469) Italian
Seven Saints
late 1450s?

The good are vulnerable
As any bird in flight,
They do not think of safety,
Are blind to possible extinction
And when most vulnerable
Are most themselves.
The good are real as the sun,
Are best perceived through clouds
Of casual corruption
That cannot kill the luminous sufficiency
That shines on city, sea and wilderness,
Fastidiously revealing
One man to another,
Who yet will not accept
Responsibilities of light.
The good incline to praise,
To have the knack of seeing that
The best is not destroyed
Although forever threatened.
The good go naked in all weathers,
And by their nakedness rebuke
The small protective sanities

That hide men from themselves.
The good are difficult to see
Though open, rare, destructible;
Always, they retain a kind of youth,
The vulnerable grace
Of any bird in flight,
Content to be itself,
Accomplished master and potential victim,
Accepting what the earth or sky intends.
I think that I know one or two
Among my friends.

The Good,
BRENDAN KENNELLY, 1967

111

PIETRO DA CORTONA (1596–1669) Italian
Saint Cecilia
1620–25

From harmony, from heav'nly harmony
    This universal frame began:
    When Nature underneath a heap
      Of jarring atoms lay,
    And could not heave her head,
The tuneful voice was heard from high:
    'Arise, ye more than dead.'
Then cold, and hot, and moist, and dry,

In order to their stations leap,
    And Music's pow'r obey.
From harmony, from heav'nly harmony
    This universal frame began:
    From harmony to harmony
Thro' all the compass of the notes it ran,
The diapason closing full in Man.

When passion cannot Music raise and quell!
    When Jubal struck the corded shell,
    His list'ning brethren stood around,
    And, wond'ring, on their faces fell
    To worship that celestial sound.
Less than a god they thought there could not dwell
    Within the hollow of that shell
    That spoke so sweetly and so well,
What passion cannot Music raise and quell!

113

The Trumpet's loud clangour
    Excites us to arms,
With shrill notes of anger,
    And mortal alarms.
The double double double beat
    Of the thund'ring Drum
Cries: 'Hark! the foes come;
Charge, charge, 't is too late to retreat.'
    The soft complaining Flute
    In dying notes discovers
    The woes of hopeless lovers,
Whose dirge is whisper'd by the warbling Lute.

    Sharp Violins proclaim
Their jealous pangs, and desperation,
Fury, frantic indignation,
Depth of pains, and height of passion,
    For the fair, disdainful dame.

    But O! what art can teach,
    What human voice can reach,
The sacred Organ's praise?
    Notes inspiring holy love,
Notes that wing their heav'nly ways
    To mend the choirs above.

Orpheus could lead the savage race;
And trees uprooted left their place,
    Sequacious of the lyre;
But bright Cecilia rais'd the wonder high'r:
When to her Organ vocal breath was giv'n,
And angel heard, and straight appear'd,
    Mistaking earth for heav'n.

As from the pow'r of sacred lays
    The spheres began to move,
And sung the great Creator's praise
    To all the blest above;
So, when the last and dreadful hour
This crumbling pageant shall devour,
The Trumpet shall be heard on high,
The dead shall live, the living die,
And Music shall untune the sky.

from *A Song for St Cecilia's Day*
JOHN DRYDEN, 1687

117

PISANELLO (about 1395–probably 1455) Italian
The Vision of Saint Eustace
mid-15th century

Let man and beast appear before him, and magnify his
    name together.
Let Noah and his company approach the throne of Grace
    and do homage to the Ark of their Salvation.
Let Abraham present a Ram, and worship the God of his
    Redemption.
Let Isaac, the Bridegroom, kneel with his Camels, and bless
    the hope of his pilgrimage.
Let Jacob, and his speckled Drove adore the good Shepherd
    of Israel.
Let Esau offer a scape Goat for his seed…
Let Nimrod, the mighty hunter, bind a Leopard to the
    altar…

Let Daniel come forth with a Lion, and praise God…
Let Naphthali with an Hind give glory…
Let Aaron, the high priest, sanctify a Bull…

Let Abiathar with a Fox praise the name of the Lord…
Let Moses, the Man of God, bless with a Lizard, in the sweet
    majesty of good-nature, and magnanimity of meekness.
Let Joshua praise God with an Unicorn…

Let David bless with the Bear...
Let Solomon praise with the Ant...

Let Tobias bless Charity with his Dog...
Let Anna bless God with the Cat...
Let Benaiah praise with the Asp...
Let Barzillai bless with the Snail...
Let Joab with the Horse worship the Lord God of Hosts
Let Shemaiah bless God with the Caterpillar...

Let Iddo praise the Lord with the Moth—the writings of
    man perish as the garment, but the Book of God
    endureth for ever.
Let Nebuchadnezzar bless with the Grasshopper—the pomp
    and vanities of the World are as the herb of the field,
    but the glory of the Lord increaseth for ever.

from *Jubilate Agno*,
CHRISTOPHER SMART, 1759–63

123

GIOVANNI DI PAOLO (active by 1417; died 1482) Italian
Saint John the Baptist retiring to the Desert
probaby about 1453

The last and greatest herald of heaven's king,
Girt with rough skins, hies to the deserts wild,
Among that savage brood the woods forth bring
Which he than man more harmless found and mild:

His food was locusts, and what young doth spring,
With honey that from virgin hives distilled;
Parched body, hollow eyes, some uncouth thing
Made him appear long since from earth exiled.

There burst he forth: 'All ye, whose hopes rely
On God, with me amidst these deserts mourn;
Repent, repent, and from old errors turn.'
Who listened to his voice, obeyed his cry?

    Only the echoes which he made relent,
    Rung from their marble caves, *Repent, repent*.

St John the Baptist,
WILLIAM DRUMMOND, early 17th century

127

GAROFALO (about 1476–1559) Italian
*Saint Augustine with the Holy Family and Saint Catherine
of Alexandria ('The Vision of Saint Augustine')*
about 1520

Blessed are all thy Saints, O God and King, who have
travelled over the tempestuous sea of this mortal life, and
have made the harbour of peace and felicity. Watch over us
who are still in our dangerous voyage; and remember such as
lie exposed to the rough storms of trouble and temptations.
Frail is our vessel, and the ocean is wide; but as in thy mercy
thou hast set our course, so steer the vessel of our life
toward the everlasting shore of peace, and bring us at length
to the quiet haven of our heart's desire, where thou, O our
God, are blessed, and livest and reignest for ever and ever.

from *The Confessions of Saint Augustine*,
SAINT AUGUSTINE, about 400

129

131

CARLO CRIVELLI
(about 1430/5–about 1494) Italian
The Annunciation, with Saint Emidius
1486

A trapped bird
A wrecked ship
An empty cup
A withered tree
Is he
Who scorns the will of the King above.

Pure gold
Bright sun
Filled wine-cup
Happy beautiful holy
Is he
Who does the will of the King of love.

The Holy Man,
BRENDAN KENNELLY, 1968

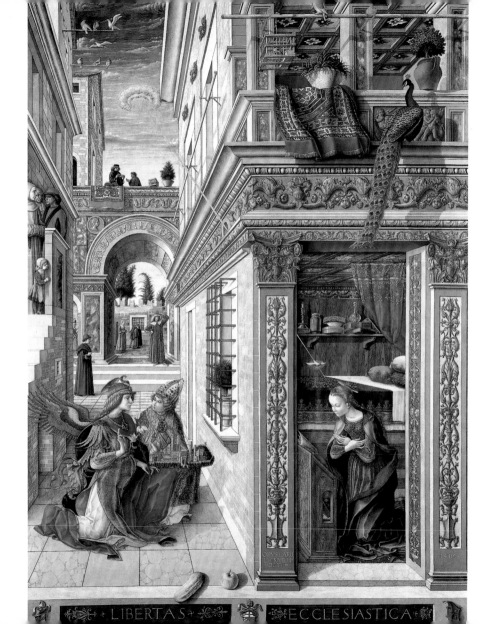

LIBERTAS · ECCLESIASTICA

135

137

ARTISTS & PAINTINGS

ANGELICO, Fra
Christ Glorified in the Court of Heaven
tempera on poplar,
32 x 73 cm, p.70

ANTONELLO da Messina
Attributed,
The Virgin and Child
oil on wood, painted surface
43.2 x 34.3 cm, p.77

BALDUNG Grien, Hans
The Trinity and Mystic Pietà
oil on oak,
112.3 x 89.1 cm, p.65

BAROCCI, Federico
The Madonna and Child with Saint Joseph and the Infant Baptist (La Madonna del Gatto)
oil on canvas,
112.7 x 92.7 cm, p.54

BAYEU y Subias, Francisco
Saint James being visited by the Virgin with a Statue of the Madonna of the Pillar
oil on canvas,
53 x 84 cm, p.74

BOTTICELLI, Sandro
'Mystic Nativity'
oil on canvas,
108.6 x 74.9 cm, p.11

BOTTICINI, Francesco
The Assumption of the Virgin
tempera on wood,
228.6 x 377.2 cm, p.37

CARAVAGGIO, Michelangelo Merisi da
The Supper at Emmaus
oil and egg (identified) on canvas,
141 x 196.2 cm, p.44

CHAMPAIGNE, Philippe de
The Vision of Saint Joseph
oil on canvas,
208.9 x 155.6 cm, p.25

CORTONA, Pietro da
Saint Cecilia
oil (identified) on canvas,
143.5 x 108.9 cm, p.113

COSTA, Lorenzo
The Adoration of the Shepherds with Angels
oil on wood,
52.4 x 37.5 cm, p.41

CRIVELLI, Carlo
The Annunciation, with Saint Emidius
egg and oil (identified) on canvas, transferred from wood,
207 x 146.7 cm, p.135

DUCCIO
The Annunciation
egg (identified) on poplar, painted surface
43 x 44 cm, p.17

ELSHEIMER, Adam
After,
Tobias and the Archangel Raphael returning with the Fish
oil on copper,
19.3 x 27.6 cm, p.29

GAROFALO
Saint Augustine and the Holy Family and Saint Catherine of Alexandria ('The Vision of Saint Augustine')
oil on wood,
64.5 x 81.9 cm, p.129

GEERTGEN TOT SINT JANS
The Nativity, at Night
oil on oak,
34.3 x 25.1 cm, p.47

GIOVANNI, di Paolo
Saint John the Baptist
retiring to the Desert
tempera on poplar,
31.1 x 38.8 cm, p.124

GOSSAERT, Jan
The Adoration of the Kings
oil (identified) on wood,
177.2 x 161.3 cm, p.50

GUERCINO
The Angel Appearing to
Hagar and Ishmael
oil on canvas,
193 x 229 cm,
Collection of Sir Dennis
Mahon, on loan to the
National Gallery, London p.8

LEONARDO da Vinci,
Associate of,
An Angel in Red with a Lute
oil (identified) on poplar,
118.8 x 61 cm, p.21

LIPPI, Fra Filippo
Seven Saints
tempera on wood,
68 x 151.5 cm, p.108

MARGARITO of Arezzo
The Virgin and Child
Enthroned, with Scenes
of the Nativity and the Lives
of the Saints
tempera on wood,
including frame
92.5 x 183 cm, p.88

PISANELLO
The Vision of Saint Eustace
tempera on wood,
54.5 x 65.5 cm, p.118

POUSSIN, Nicolas
The Annunciation
oil on canvas,
105.8 x 103.9 cm, p.82

PROVOOST, Jan
Attributed,
The Virgin and Child
in a Landscape
oil on oak,
60.3 x 50.2 cm, p.90

RENI, Guido
Christ embracing Saint John
the Baptist
oil (identified) on canvas,
48.5 x 68.5 cm, p.61

The Coronation of the Virgin
oil on copper,
66.6 x 48.8 cm, p.101

UCCELLO, Paolo
Saint George and the Dragon
oil on canvas,
56.5 x 74 cm, p.104

VALDES LEAL, Juan de
The Immaculate Conception
of the Virgin, with Two
Donors
oil on canvas,
189.7 x 204.5 cm, p.97

THE WILTON DIPTYCH
Richard II presented to the
Virgin and Child by his
Patron Saint John the
Baptist and Saints Edward
and Edmund
egg (identified) on oak,
each wing
53 x 37 cm, p.33

WRITERS & WORKS

ACKNOWLEDGMENTS

The editor and publishers gratefully acknowledge permission to reprint copyright material below. Every effort has been made to contact the original copyright holders of the material included. Any omissions will be rectified in future editions.

The Holy Man by Brendan Kennelly from 'Love of Ireland' published by Mercier Press by permission of the author and publisher.

The Good by Brendan Kennelly from 'Breathing Spaces' published by Bloodaxe Books by permission of the author and publisher.

Meeting with a Stranger by James Kirkup by kind permission of James Kirkup and Oxford University Press. The poem first appeared in the poet's collection 'The Submerged Village' (1951) and was reprinted in his 'Collected Shorter Poems' volume 1; 'Omens of Disaster' by Salzburg University Press.

Our Lady of Walsingham, The Quaker Graveyard of Nantucket by Robert Lowell from 'Selected Poems' by Robert Lowell published Faber & Faber Ltd. by permission of the publisher.

Our Lady of Walsingham, The Quaker Graveyard of Nantucket from 'Lord Weary's Castle', copyright 1946 and renewed 1974 by Robert Lowell, reprinted by permission of Harcourt Brace & Co.

The Annunciation by Edwin Muir from 'Collected Poems' by Edwin Muir published by Faber & Faber Ltd. by permission of the publisher.

The Annunciation by Edwin Muir from 'Collected Poems' by Edwin Muir. Copyright © 1980 by Willa Muir. Used by permission of Oxford University Press, Inc.

The Plain Facts by Ruth Pitter. Copyright © Mark Pitter by permission of Mark Pitter.

On the Marriage of a Virgin by Dylan Thomas from 'Collected Poems: 1934–1952 published by J.M. Dent & Sons Ltd by permission of David Higham Associates.

On the Marriage of a Virgin by Dylan Thomas from 'The Poems of Dylan Thomas'. Copyright © 1943 by New Directions Publishing Corp. Reprinted by permission of New Directions Publishing Corp.

excerpt from *War and Peace* by Leo Tolstoy translated by Constance Garnett by kind permission of A. P. Watt Ltd. on behalf of the Executors of the estate of Constance Garnett.

The Magi by William Butler Yeats from 'The Collected Poems of W. B. Yeats' by permission of A. P. Watt Ltd. on behalf of Michael Yeats.

Title page: Garafolo, detail of
*Saint Augustine and the
Holy Family and Saint
Catherine of Alexandria*, ('The
Vision of Saint Augustine')
about 1520

Messengers of Grace title page:
Guercino, *The Angel
Appearing to Hagar and
Ishmael*, 1652–53, Collection of
Sir Dennis Mahon, on loan to the
National Gallery, London

The Light of the World title page:
Michelangelo Merisi da
Caravaggio, *The Supper at
Emmaus*, 1601

Queen of Heaven title page:
Francisco Bayeu y Subias,
*Saint James being visited by
the Virgin with a Statue of the
Madonna of the Pillar*, 1760

Saints title page: Paolo Uccello,
Saint George and the Dragon,
about 1460